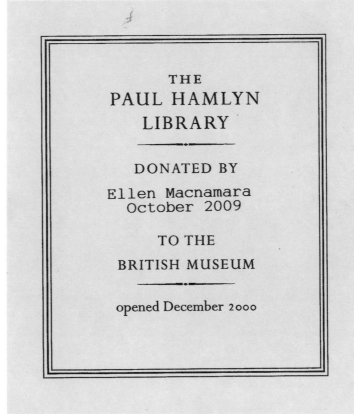

CITIES OF
ANCIENT GREECE AND ITALY:
PLANNING IN CLASSICAL ANTIQUITY

CITIES OF ANCIENT GREECE AND ITALY: PLANNING IN CLASSICAL ANTIQUITY

J.B. WARD-PERKINS

Ellen Macnama

 SIDGWICK & JACKSON LONDON

First published in Great Britain in 1974

Originally published in USA by George Braziller Inc., and
in Canada by Doubleday Canada, Limited

ISBN 0 283 98266 7

Printed in Great Britain by
Lewis Reprints Ltd.
member of Brown Knight & Truscott Group
London and Tonbridge
for Sidgwick & Jackson Limited
1 Tavistock Chambers, Bloomsbury Way,
London, WC1A 2SG

CONTENTS

PREFACE

Of the many possible approaches to the study of the classical city and its planning I have chosen in the pages that follow to concentrate upon the element of formal planning in classical urban design.

This for several reasons. For one thing, it is this field in which the archaeological discoveries of the last few decades have most radically altered traditional perspectives. Scholars in the past have tended to approach the subject in terms of Greek or of Roman practice, or at best of an emphasis upon the difference between the two. To the extent that these were the product of differing historical circumstances and sensibilities, this approach is a perfectly valid one; but it has undoubtedly had the effect of obscuring the basic fact that in this, as in so much else, Greece and Rome represent two phases of the same great experiment in human living.

Another reason is that Greece invented, and through Rome bequeathed to ourselves, a concept of planning which is now so familiar that it is hard to remember that it was once new. Although Egypt and many of the ancient civilizations of the Near East possessed the architectural and surveying skills needed for the laying out of a city, they preferred (to use Paul Lampl's phrase) to work "from the inside outwards." Even a city such as Akhenaten's new capital of Tell el-Amarna was in essence an aggregate of its component units, its formal planning being virtually limited to the laying out of the main street and the zoning of its various quarters. It was left to the rationally minded Greeks to evolve a system of planning "from the outside inwards," a system in which the city itself was the formal planning unit within which the individual buildings had to find their appropriate place.

It only remains to express my deep indebtedness to such previous writers on this subject as Ferdinando Castagnoli and Roland Martin; to all those scholars whose recent work in this field has so notably enlarged our range of knowledge; and to the many friends who by discussion, by the provision of illustration, or in other ways have contributed so much to the completion of this book.

J.B.W.-P.

British School at Rome

1. INTRODUCTION

Greece and Rome were both essentially urban civilizations. To the Greek citizen of the classical city-state the *polis* was the self-evident expression of a way of life, an all-embracing attitude to man and his environment of which our word "politics" expresses only one of many related aspects; and although the events of the following centuries were in fact to reveal the fatal political weaknesses of this conception, it was still through the cities which they found or created that Alexander the Great's successors ruled their vast kingdoms. To the Roman of the Empire, faced by the same problems on an even larger scale, the city was still the natural unit of local administration, the most tangible and direct point of contact between ruler and ruled. Where city life on the Mediterranean pattern did not already exist, everything possible was done to create it, and as much as any other single factor it was the slow breakdown of urban prosperity under the twin burden of warfare and taxation that brought about the final downfall of Roman rule. The history of the classical town is in a very real sense the history of classical civilization itself.

Although this study of classical town planning concerns itself very largely with the formal layouts which are its most tangible surviving expression, it is well to remember that this was not by any means the aspect of urban planning that bulked largest in the eyes of its contemporaries. Questions of formal layout seem in fact to have been very largely ignored or taken for granted by most Greek writers, or considered if at all for their relevance to the political and social problems which were their main interest. Plato's and Aristotle's discussions of the ideal city are concerned almost entirely with such matters as the proportions and relationships of different social classes, and only marginally with questions of urban layout or physical organization. Not until Hellenistic Greek times were there the beginnings of a professional, technical literature, and not until Roman times did such matters become a proper matter for the attention of men of the social standing of Pliny and Frontinus, or of such serious and widely read writers as Varro and Vitruvius. Even so the only substantial body of technical literature that has come down to us concerns such related subjects as field survey and water supply. For town planning as such we are driven very largely to the study of surviving remains.

Fortunately these remains are both numerous and articulate. In no field has air photography, supported by excavation, made a greater contribution to knowledge. If today we can afford to be critical of opinions held by eminent scholars of the recent past, it is very largely because we possess vastly more evidence than they did. The most conspicuous victim of these new perspectives has been the notion that orthogonal schemes of town planning, i.e. gridded schemes based on the intersection of streets at right angles, were invented independently in Greece and Italy. There were indeed important differences between Greek and Roman planning, but, as we shall see, they have to be studied within the framework of a single, organically developing tradition.

One of the aspects of the subject which air photography brings vividly before us is the distinction between communities that were planned and those which, like Topsy, "just growed." For every center of human habitation planned and laid out on some particular historical occasion, there were half-a-dozen others that grew up where and as they did without benefit of formal planning. Springs, river crossings, harbors, crossroads, natural fortresses—these are only some of the features around which human beings have at all times tended to congregate in the course of their everyday affairs; and what the resulting settlements lack in planning they often make up for in the vitality which may so easily elude the planner.[1]

The fact that almost every city of substance contains elements both of planned and of spontaneous growth must never be allowed to obscure the fundamental nature of this distinction, which is one that leaves an almost indelible imprint upon all later development. The pages that follow are concerned mainly with those elements that reveal conscious planning. But even here one does well to remember that such planning is often no more than a formalization and rationalization of earlier, less studied practices. The institutions and the buildings for which the founders of the new cities of classical antiquity had to provide were those which had grown up over the years, in the older, freely developing communities. Even the rare moments of pure invention were loaded with the experience of the past. Divorced of its roots in the society which it served, the study of ancient city planning becomes an arid exercise, devoid of historical significance.

2. ARCHAIC GREECE AND THE BEGINNING OF CITY PLANNING

The Greek city of the classical age did not develop in isolation. The Aegean world of the Bronze-Age Minoan and Mycenaean civilizations had a highly sophisticated architecture, known to us both from the accounts that have come down to us, filtered through the folk memory of the Homeric poems, and from its excavated remains at Knossos, Mycenae, and elsewhere. Further afield there were the ancient civilizations of the Near East, in Mesopotamia and Egypt, to both of which Bronze-Age and classical Greece alike owed a great deal.

Of the two, the Aegean Bronze Age—though in its later phases the work of a people who were ancestral to the historical Greeks—has only a very limited bearing upon the urban forms current in the classical age. For one thing the Minoan and Mycenaean civilizations were essentially aristocratic in their organization. In marked contrast to classical Greece, the outstanding monuments are the palaces and the country residences of the ruling classes, and it was these that attracted the ingenuity and skills which a later age was to lavish on public architecture and planning. For anything comparable to the water supply and drainage systems of Knossos we have to turn to classical Etruria and later still to Rome (p. 34). By comparison with the palace, the ordinary domestic and artisan quarters of a small Late-Minoan town such as Gournia, in eastern Crete (Fig. 1), are mere agglomerations of rooms and courtyards ranged haphazardly along the winding alleyways that encircle the central residence, like a small medieval town clinging to the skirts of some baronial castle. (At Karphi, also in eastern Crete (Fig. 2), one sees how this same tradition disintegrated when deprived of the central unifying element which the palace afforded.) Furthermore, the thread of continuity from the Bronze-Age past was everywhere very tenuous. Agamemnon's Mycenae and Nestor's Pylos lay sacked and derelict, while the last and most destructive wave of Greek-speaking invaders, the Dorians, were slowly re-evolving the basis of a comparable but in detail very different civilization. Athens, where the palace of a Mycenaean ruler developed without any appreciable break into the nucleus of the later Greek city, was exceptional in this respect. There may have been some elements of architectural continuity. The close resemblance between the earliest known Greek temples and the Mycenaean *megaron* can hardly be accidental, and the classical stoa too may have Minoan precedents.[2] But these were individual building types. Of the urban settings (such as they were) of an earlier age little or nothing seems to have survived across the intervening darkness.

The one possible exception is in the Greek colonies of Ionia, along the western fringes of Asia Minor. These were established in the tenth century B.C. by Ionian Greek refugees from the mainland, fleeing before the Dorians. From their old homes the Ionian settlers carried with them whatever still survived of Mycenaean civilization. It was in Ionia that the tales of the heroic past took shape as the Homeric epic, and here if anywhere one may one day hope to find tangible evidence of the sort of architectural continuity hinted at by the forms of the earliest Greek temples.

There were also new factors at work. In their new homes the Greek settlers found themselves once more in contact with the rich civilizations of the ancient East, at first through the native kingdoms of Asia Minor and later through direct commerce with Cyprus, Egypt, and the Levant. At first sight the cities of the ancient East might seem to have had little to inspire the urban planner. Most of them were the product of centuries of unplanned, accreted growth, within which any element of monumentality and formal planning was reserved for the palaces and temples that were ruthlessly inserted into or on top of the existing urban framework. No Greek ever saw the Egyptian workmen's villages at Kāhūn and at Tell el-Amarna,[3] with their rows of uniform barrack blocks and parallel streets framed within rigidly rectangular enclosures. But across the centuries these find their counterpart in the orderly cantonments of the Roman quarry workers at Simitthu in North Africa,[4] and they illustrate vividly the fund of practical planning experience that was already in circulation in Egypt, awaiting concrete expression whenever an appropriate occasion presented itself. Further afield, in Mesopotamia, the Assyrians were great builders of new cities, and these too were ordered, though not rigidly orthogonal, creations;[5] one recalls Herodotus's description (I,180) of Babylon as "intersected by straight streets, some parallel and some at right angles to the river." Ideas of orderly planning were in the air, and the Greeks would everywhere have found themselves exposed to the stimulus of notions which they could then develop in their own particular way. Already in the eighth century B.C., Oriental contacts and imports were everywhere shaping the emergence of the nascent classical civilization—metalwork, painting, sculpture, fabrics, handicrafts of every sort. The "Aeolic" capitals of the earliest Greek architecture in stone echoed a type that was widespread in Phoenicia and Palestine, while more generally the whole Greek architectural system of column, capital, and entablature represents the impact of the masonry architecture of the ancient East, and in particular of Egypt, upon the primitive timber and mud-brick construction of Aegean Greece. Patterns of urban life tend to be more conservative than fashions in building, but when the time did come for change, the seed was already sown.

The Greeks themselves attributed the formal schemes of orthogonal town planning with which they were familiar to Hippodamos of Miletus, who lived and worked in the fifth century B.C.; but, as we shall see later (pp. 14–17), this can only be true of certain aspects of Hippodamos's work. Already in the early seventh century B.C. Smyrna had been rebuilt, after a disastrous fire, upon a plan of which the controlling feature was a series of parallel streets running north and south. At one point an open space was reserved for the agora, and near it, on a low eminence, stood a temple.[6] The scheme is a simple one, but by contrast with what had gone before on the same site it unquestionably represents the deliberate adoption of a measure of the sort of formal planning which we shall meet again, a few years later, at Megara Hyblaea in Sicily (see p. 23).

In the long-established cities of Ionia, as of the mainland, such opportunities for radical reconstruction were not common. But these same cities were among the first to send out the colonies which were to play such an important part in carrying the Greek model of urban civilization to large areas of the Mediterranean world, from the Black Sea to the Straits of Gibraltar. The product of population pressures on a people with a genius for seafaring and commerce, the colonies were linked to their mother cities by ties of religion, interest, and sentiment; but in all other respects they were autonomous city-states, and although some may have been founded on the sites of earlier, informal trading posts, most were for all practical purposes new foundations. Most of the remains that have come down to us are inevitably those of the later, more substantial stages of their architectural history, and it is only occasionally that circumstance offers us a glimpse of one of these colonies as it was at the moment of settlement. Such glimpses do, however, support the commonsensical belief that here was the natural proving ground for whatever ideas of formal planning were available at the time of their foundation.

It was, then, renewed contact with the civilizations of the ancient East that furnished the Greeks with a fund of stimulating fresh ideas—in this as in so many other fields—and it was the requirements of the colonies overseas that gave these ideas substance and shaped their early development on Greek soil. The latter is a subject to which we shall be returning in a later chapter. But first a general word about the political and social institutions for which the Greek *polis* was expected to make provision.

Foremost among these was the *agora*. This combined the functions of a market-place, a place of assembly, and a setting for ceremonies and spectacles—the natural center for any form of civic life for which there was no other specific provision. In origin it was little more than an open space conveniently situated somewhere near the center of the town, but in course of time there grew up around it such buildings as the meeting place of the city council (*bouleuterion*), the offices of the individual magistrates, temples and altars, fountain houses, law courts, and covered halls (*stoai*) for the use of citizens and merchants. Some of the activities so represented might eventually move to more convenient homes elsewhere in the city, as for example at Athens to the Theater of Dionysus or to the meeting place of the assembly on the Pnyx. But the agora remained the heart of the city and the focus of civic activity.

In this respect the agora took the place which at a more primitive stage had been occupied by the acropolis and the palace of the king. This again is well illustrated at Athens, where, since Mycenaean times, the Acropolis had been the residence of the ruler, the seat of the palace cult, and a place of refuge in times of trouble. The cult remained there throughout antiquity, dominating the city. But at a very early date the center of gravity, including the busy artisan and residential quarters, began to creep westwards and northwards, over the slopes of the Areopagus and along the network of winding roads that led out into the open countryside. As late as the seventh century B.C. the basin of lower ground to the northwest of the Acropolis was still the potters' quarter—the Kerameikos—and still in active use as a cemetery. Then, at the very end of the century, a nucleus of public buildings began to take shape along the western side of the basin, facing eastwards across the very ancient road that skirted the foot of the low hill of Kolonos. By the end of the sixth century the open ground to the east of the road had been drained and water supplied to a large public fountain; and during the following centuries the whole area gradually took architectural shape by the addition of buildings along the remaining three sides (Figs. 3–5). Between them these added buildings, and in particular the great stoas, came in time to give the whole a certain monumental unity. But this unity was the product of piecemeal growth over the years, not of prior planning. Architectural congruity was achieved only by the extraordinary conservatism of Greek taste in such matters as the use of materials and of such architectural stereotypes as the classical orders and the pedimental facade, a conservatism that was coupled with a rare sensitivity in matters of scale and siting. The same conservatism was evident also in the choice of certain established building types to satisfy certain specific requirements. The following are a few of those which were to become an essential part of the vocabulary of any Greek city planner.

The Greek temple is a type too familiar to call for further comment. Another very familiar type is the theater, with its rising circular tiers of seats and exiguous stage building. Its positioning within the city was very largely determined by the terrain, since it was not until Roman times that the seating began to be built up on massive substructures. The council building (*bouleuterion*) may conveniently be described as a theaterlike place of assembly in which the seating has been enclosed within the four walls of a gabled rectangular hall. As life became more sophisticated, many of the other civic activities which had formerly taken place in the open air were given similar shelter. One of the most characteristic of all Greek building types, the *stoa*, was in essence no more than a roofed extension of the agora, in the form of a colonnaded portico. Simple timber porticoes of this type are attested as early as the seventh century at Larisa-on-the-Hermos, and the following centuries saw their steady development both in materials and in design, through the introduction of such features as inner colonnades, projecting wings, rows of shops, and, by Hellenistic times, upper stories. The restored Stoa of Attalos (Fig. 6) in the Agora at Athens gives an excellent idea of Greek urban architecture at its most grandiose.

Of the essential institutions of the Greek *polis* only the gymnasium, the educational and cultural as well as the athletic center of the city, was a latecomer to urban planning. The three great philosophical schools at Athens (from which we inherit the words "academy," "cynic," and the French "lycée") took their names from the suburbs in which they were located: Plato's academy in Akademe, Aristotle and the Peripatetics at Lykeion, Antisthenes and the Cynics at Kynosarges. Not until the fourth century (Priene, Alexandria, Megalopolis) did the gymnasium begin to take formal shape as a fully urban institution.

3. HIPPODAMOS AND THE CLASSICAL GREEK CITY

Hippodamos, whom the later Greeks credited with the invention of the formal city planning with which they were familiar, was born in Miletus, probably in the closing years of the sixth century. From Aristotle, our fullest source, we learn that "he invented the divisions of cities by classes"; also that he was eccentric in his appearance and habits and that he was a political theorist who wrote a treatise on the ideal constitution. Although his only specifically attested work as a planner is the laying out of Peiraeus—the harbor town of Athens—at some date during the second quarter of the fifth century, he is known to have taken part in the foundation of the colony of Thurii in southern Italy in 444–3 B.C., and it is a reasonable assumption that he played a leading part in the planning of it. It is likely, though unproven, that as a young man he participated in the refoundation of Miletus after the defeat of the Persians in 479. On the other hand Strabo's statement that he was responsible for the plan of Rhodes, founded in 408–7 B.C., must be mistaken, although it is good evidence both of his later reputation and of the essentially "Hippodamian" character of the new foundation.[7]

It will be seen that, for all his later fame, Hippodamos is an elusive figure. Inventor or codifier? Practical planner or theoretician? Before trying to answer these questions, let us look briefly at a few of the best-attested examples of classical Greek planning.

One starts almost inevitably with Miletus (Figs. 7–11). Excavation has revealed a rigidly orthogonal plan, based on two distinct, but seemingly contemporary, grids of uniform housing blocks, separated from each other by an irregular zone of public buildings. The principle of the layout, a repeated pattern of identical units, is childishly simple. Its subtleties lay almost exclusively in the application of this simple scheme to the terrain. Ample space was left (Fig. 8) for the development of the city's mercantile, civic, and religious institutions—each in clear, functional relationship to the harbors, to the domestic quarters, and to the city's landward communications. The very modest provision for temples is partly explained by the fact that the Milesians' great sanctuary, the Didymaion, lay some miles outside the city, to the south. A feature that distinguishes this from most Greek plans is the very limited use of wider, arterial avenues—only one in the north quarter and two in the south. The fact that the fifth-century defenses enclosed, but were not organically related to, the inhabited area is, on the other hand, characteristic of Greek planning at all periods.

This was an ambitious plan, and many generations were to pass before it could be fully taken up. But as the city prospered and grew, so its various parts were able to develop freely and easily within the framework that had been prepared for them. The first area to be developed architecturally was the North Agora. Figure 9 shows this as it appeared at the end of the fourth century. A long stoa, with offices or magazines opening off it, fronted on to the harbor. Attached to it in the rear was a square colonnaded court, and behind this a large public building, perhaps the *prytaneion* (for public hospitality). A short projecting wing at the west end of the stoa balanced the enclosure of the shrine of Apollo Delphinios. The South Agora did not take shape until the following century (Fig. 10), in this case as a vast, near-symmetrical, rectangular open space framed by stoas. To the north of it lay the council chamber (*bouleuterion*), added between 175 and 164 B.C.; the open space linking the two agoras was given architectural shape by a southward extension of the North Agora buildings and the addition, opposite it, of a gymnasium. In all of this one can detect two complementary tendencies. One (which reached full fruition only in the Roman period) was towards the development of significant architectural relationships between the individual public buildings, which initially had been treated as virtually independent units, well sited for convenience of use but with little or no sense of any broader visual unities. The other was the emergence of a certain feeling for symmetry, notably in the development of the U-shaped stoas so characteristic of later Hellenistic planning; but the symmetry is never forced, and there is a studied avoidance of axial monumentality. This sort of layout was the natural, almost inevitable, result of adapting such familiar building types as the stoa to the framework established by the initial orthogonal plan. It was functional, effective, at times rather dull, but with the saving virtue of good manners, thanks to the consistent use of traditional materials within a broadly conservative architectural tradition.

For a picture of the domestic quarter of one of these planned Greek cities we have to turn to Olynthus or Priene. At Olynthus, an ancient hilltop city of typically irregular plan in northern Greece, a spacious new quarter was laid out about 432 B.C., with several broad avenues running north and south, intersected at regular intervals by numerous smaller cross streets running east and west. The individual blocks measured 120 by 300 Attic feet, and each contained ten houses of equal size, laid out, five and five, with a narrow alleyway between (Figs. 11, 11a). Although no two houses are exactly alike, all conform to a recognizable type, with the main rooms facing south across a courtyard. At Priene (Figs. 12, 12a, 12b) the blocks measured 120 by 160 feet, and the individual houses, initially planned as four to a block, were far more varied. The overall plan, though based on the same principles, could hardly have been more different in its effect. Built about the middle of the fourth century on the steep lower slopes of Mount Micale, it illustrated how ingeniously and attractively orthogonal "gridiron" planning could be applied to a highly improbable site. Many of the cross streets were steep flights of steps, but there was excellent east-to-west communication along the slopes, the principal streets being wider than the rest. (There are many analogies here with sixteenth-century Valletta.) The agora occupied a central terraced area, overlooking the gymnasium (for which space was reserved outside the formal layout, just inside the walls), and it was itself overlooked by the splendidly sited Temple of Athena and by the theater. Behind these again the acropolis, towering 1,000 feet above, formed a magnificent backdrop. As at Miletus, the defenses were quite independent of the street plan.[8]

Rhodes (Fig. 13) and Knidos represent two other well-attested examples of classical Greek planning. Rhodes, founded in 408–7 B.C., is another instance of an ambitious orthogonal layout based on broad avenues (in one case 16 meters wide) which intersect to form 600-foot squares, which in turn were subdivided by narrower streets into smaller, rectangular blocks. The site chosen, ringed with hills and shelving down towards the harbors, embraced more than two kilometers of formal layout in either direction, with the city blocks terraced up the slopes like the seats of a theater.[9] An elaborate system of street drainage, if original, is the earliest attested example of its type in the Greek world. Knidos, just across the water from Rhodes and perhaps half a century later, is in plan a bigger and better Priene, with the sea thrown in for good measure. Between them Rhodes and Knidos exemplify the best of "Hippodamian" planning, making full use of the visual possibilities of a varied terrain but as yet unaffected by the more flexible schemes discussed in the next chapter, of which Pergamon is the outstanding surviving representative.

And where does Hippodamos himself stand in all this? The main lines of the planning formula which antiquity associated with his name are clear enough, as exemplified at Olynthus, Priene, Knidos, and Rhodes (but not, ironically, at Miletus, the almost-square, checkerboard scheme of which is uncharacteristic of Greek planning). He certainly did not invent it, but he may well have rationalized and codified it. Nor must one overlook the evidence of Aristotle, cited above. A constitutional theorist who, in the best tradition of Ionian speculative science and philosophy, "invented the divisions of cities by classes" was surely quite as much concerned with the physical expression of political and social needs as with geometry and landscaping. His one certainly attested work, the laying out of Peiraeus, the port of Athens, after the Persian Wars, does in fact appear to have been primarily a work of zoning. The area is overlaid with modern building, but by a happy chance it has yielded, in addition to traces of orthogonal street planning, a large number of official boundary stones (*horoi*). The first and epigraphically earlier series delimits the several areas reserved for public use: the commercial port (*emporion*), the military port, and such other public utilities as the agora and religious sanctuaries. This is followed by a series representative of the individual buildings which in due course were erected within these areas.

The colony of Thurii, in the foundation of which Hippodamos participated, was unusual in being drawn from many parts of Greece, rather than from a single city, and it is a reasonable guess that the element of idealism and its resulting problems appealed to Hippodamos, who must surely have taken an active part in the initial planning. The establishment of the colony is described in some detail by Diodorus (XII,10): the ritual consultation of the oracle (religion); the location of a spring (water supply); the building around it of a wall (defense); the laying out of a grid of broad avenues (*plateiai*)—four in one direction and three others at right angles to them (primary zoning); and finally the development of this scheme by the building of houses, served by lesser streets (*stenōpoi*).[10] Nothing is said specifically of the reservation of public land within the city nor—except by implication in the terms of the oracle—of the division of the lands outside it, but otherwise this is a remarkably explicit statement of the priorities and procedures of the building of a new Greek city.

What legislation was there to order and to maintain such a city? From a very early date every city must have had laws regulating such matters as public and private property, but (such being the Greek temperament) no two were exactly alike. Nevertheless, just as the fifth century saw the emergence of a widely accepted norm of "Hippodamian" planning practice, to be applied as local circumstance dictated, so the works of Plato and Aristotle reflect at a theoretical level the emergence in contemporary usage of certain widely accepted principles and practices. Among these we find a basic distinction between public and private property (often including a right of expropriation when in the public interest); the nomination of magistrates (usually called *astynomoi*) to supervise the public domain, including such vital services as streets, water supply and drainage; other magistrates (*agoranomoi*) to supervise the markets and other commercial activities; sometimes an architect to maintain public buildings (as distinct from the erection of new buildings, which were usually the object of special legislation); and a mass of detailed provisions regulating the uses and abuses of private property. Among the surviving texts there is one that sets out in extraordinary detail the functions of the *astynomoi* of Hellenistic Pergamon.[11] Another records the procedures for a formal enlargement of the city of Colophon in Ionia in the late fourth century B.C.[12]: the nomination of a supervisory commission, the performance of religious rites, the preparation of plans for the new walls, the choice of an architect to build them and to lay out the new street plan, the raising of funds, the reservation of "a site for the agora, for the workshops, and for all necessary public land," and provision for the sale of the remainder. So much of our knowledge comes inevitably from the study of the monuments that it is all the more precious when the curtain lifts briefly to reveal something of the attitudes and preoccupations of the men who built them.

4. THE CITIES OF HELLENISTIC ASIA MINOR AND SYRIA

The meteoric career of Alexander the Great left an indelible mark on every aspect of the political, social, and economic life of his time. The familiar world of the self-contained city-state was dead. Men were faced with vast new horizons, new commercial opportunities and markets, new social and religious problems and preoccupations. Prominent among the latter was the mutual influence of Greek thought and ways and those of the time-old cultures of the ancient East. Nothing could ever be quite the same again.

Town planning was no exception. Within the resulting development one can distinguish two broadly contrasting currents. One, rooted in the long-standing Hellenistic traditions of Asia Minor and outstandingly exemplified by Attalid Pergamon, was an ultimate monumentalization of the old, freely developing Greek city, with or without benefit of the currently fashionable "Hippodamian" practices. The other, represented in the new Greek cities that were everywhere established in the freshly conquered lands of Egypt, Syria, and beyond, embodied the accumulated experience of centuries of colonization among alien peoples. Inevitably the two currents were to meet and mingle, and at the level of their individual component elements they already had a great deal in common, but in terms of the total resulting effect they are poles apart.

Pergamon is one of the most extraordinary success stories of antiquity. Out of the political turmoil following Alexander's death in 323 B.C. it emerged during the third century as the capital of a powerful kingdom and, notably under Eumenes II (197–159 B.C.), was one of the major artistic centers of the Hellenistic world. The site is a magnificent one—a detached, elongated eminence, defended on three sides by plunging slopes and only on the fourth side shelving more gently down from the citadel at the north end towards the plain of the river Kaikos, some 900 feet below. The Hellenistic town occupied the crest and southern slopes. A single main street wound its way from the main south gate up to the citadel. Freely grouped along it there was, on the lower slopes, a monumental, terraced quarter comprising an agora, gymnasia, and a grandiose sanctuary of Demeter; on the open middle slopes a residential quarter still largely unexcavated; and along the summit, facing out westwards across the theater, the second group of monumental, terraced structures which constitutes the upper city.

A glance at the plan of the upper city (Fig. 14) will suffice to show that, although it was not the product of a predisposed plan but of a process of progressive creation over a period of about a century (indeed the last comer, the Temple of Trajan, was added nearly 300 years later), these buildings managed to achieve a remarkable unity of architectural intent. The successive terraces grew naturally out of the landscape; the theater, the focal point of the finished design, fits, like the pivot of a fan, into a shallow natural reentrant that might have been designed for it; and—a master stroke—the long horizontal of the theater portico, with its massive buttresses, gives a solid basis and a point of reference to the steady buildup of the terraces above (Fig. 15). Greek architects had long been masters at siting individual buildings, often on dominating platforms; the Temple of Apollo at Delphi and the

Parthenon are outstanding examples. But the monumental organization of a whole complex of terraced buildings, the individual elements of which were deliberately played down so as to accentuate the organic unity of the whole—this was something quite new. The details confirm the deliberate intention of its creators: for example, the linking of the successive levels of the terraced terrain by means of porticoes of two or even three stories opening off the different levels; or again, the choice of the functional sobriety of the Doric order for all but the details of the temples and of secondary orders. This was a consciously landscaped architecture, all the more remarkable for being the creation, not of a single genius, but of a succession of anonymous working architects.

That these builders of Attalid Pergamon were the creators of such a tradition of monumentally conceived, landscaped grouping we may reasonably doubt. Perhaps it was Rhodes (see p. 15) which first turned men's thoughts in this direction. Though laid out on strict Hippodamian lines (Fig. 13), with a much-admired grid of fine avenues and streets, its adaptation to a site which Diodorus (XIX,45) likens to a theater must inevitably have involved a lot of terraced landscaping. From this it was only a step—though a vital step—to a more freely articulated sort of urbanistic landscaping, in which streets and buildings were designed to exploit and to enhance the natural movement of the terrain; and it may well be that, as Martin has suggested, this step was taken in another new city, Halicarnassos, a neighbor of Rhodes, on the mainland barely a hundred miles to the northwest. Here Maussolos, the native dynast of Caria, established his new capital in the second quarter of the fourth century B.C. The ancient buildings, alas, are gone; but one can still admire the site—a peninsular and rocky point enclosing a sheltered, semicircular bay—and we have Vitruvius's appreciative description of the skill with which Maussolos developed its natural advantages. "Like a theater," he remarks (II,8,42), with the agora at the foot, beside the harbor; crowning the right-hand point a temple of Aphrodite and Hermes, and on the promontory opposite, where now stands the splendid crusader castle, the palace of Maussolos; on the summit of the acropolis a sanctuary and a colossal statue of Ares and, halfway up the slopes, unifying the whole, a broad, curving avenue, dominated centrally by the towering bulk of the Mausoleum.

There seem to have been two distinct novelties about this creation: the one a self-conscious rationalization and extension of the innate Greek sensibility for siting individual buildings within a landscape; the other the incorporation within such a setting of a dominating, artificially sited countermotif—the Mausoleum. It is probably no accident that this was the work of a Hellenized "barbarian," the representative of a monarch in the far-off East, where there was a time-old tradition of such man-made architectural "wonders."[13] Be that as it may, the history of fourth-century and later planning in Asia Minor is very largely one of the contrapuntal development of these two themes, alongside and interwoven with that of Hippodamian planning. Aigai (Figs. 16, 17), Assos (Figs. 18, 19), Priene (Fig. 12), Alinda, Labranda, Pisidian Antioch, Sagalassos, Termessos, Kremna, Attaleia (Antalya)[14]—the mixture varies, but right down to and into Roman times these were lively, influential forces within the urban scene.

In Syria and in Egypt Alexander and his successors were faced with a very different problem. Their task was to establish centers of Greek military and political authority in lands with a long but totally alien tradition of urban civilization. Since to a Greek the city was the only thinkable Hellenic component of the creative dialogue between East and West which it was Alexander's dream to create, in almost every case the only practical solution was to establish new cities (Alexander himself is credited by Plutarch [*Alex*.I,5] with founding no less than seventy, among them Alexandria itself), and almost inevitably the models followed were those of orthodox Greek colonial planning.

They did their work well. Many of these cities have been continuously occupied ever since, and we should know little of their original layout were it not that, once established, their street plans proved remarkably tenacious and can still be determined in considerable detail by the study of their later classical or modern successors. Of the cities founded in Syria and Mesopotamia by Seleucus Nicator (312–280 B.C.), Seleucia, joint capital and successor to Babylon, still awaits exploration; but enough is known of Antioch itself, Damascus (Fig. 21—exceptionally an enlargement of an existing city), Laodiceia (Latakieh) (Fig. 20), Apamea and Beroea (Aleppo) to show that they conformed to a very simple standard type, consisting essentially of a network of uniform city blocks, each roughly twice as broad as long and set at right angles to the main axis of an orthogonal grid of streets. Open spaces were reserved for the agora and certain public buildings (at Damascus, for example, the great temple), and the whole was loosely enclosed within a circuit of walls, the siting of which was normally quite independent of the street plan. One or more of the longitudinal (and on occasion of the transverse) streets were usually wider than the rest. Such were the axial avenue of Antioch (subsequently colonnaded by Herod the Great) and "the Street called Straight" of St. Paul's Damascus (*Acts of the Apostles*, IX, 11).

For a fuller picture of one of these Seleucid cities we can fortunately turn to the remains of Dura-Europos, a fortress and commercial entrepôt on the banks of the Euphrates, midway between Seleucia and Antioch. Founded about 300 B.C. and destroyed shortly after A.D. 250, the city occupied a broad promontory of level ground which commanded both the river and the caravan route up the south bank. The initial plan (Fig. 22) was of an extreme simplicity—a grid of nine longitudinal and twelve transverse streets enclosing between sixty and seventy city blocks, each measuring 100 by 200 feet. The streets were all 18 feet wide except for one longitudinal avenue (36 feet) and the fourth and eighth transverse streets (24 feet), between which, at the center of the town, an area of eight blocks was reserved for the agora and its associated buildings. Any other public buildings were to be housed within the individual city blocks. The fortress occupied an independent bluff overlooking the river, and the city walls zigzagged along the cliffs of two steep side valleys. Only across the flat landward side did they follow an arbitrary line, and even here they were allowed to diverge slightly from the alignment of the adjoining street. The total area enclosed was about 150 acres, and except at the single landward gate the walls and street plan were distinct, uncoordinated entities.

The sudden destruction of Dura in antiquity, and its systematic excavation in modern times, afford a rare glimpse of the efficacy of the original planning. On the whole it comes well out of the test. As one would expect, the fortress and walls were promptly completed and efficiently maintained through the successive stages of Seleucid Greek, Parthian, and, for the last seventy years, Roman rule, when it housed the commander of the Euphrates river frontier and a garrison. On the civil side the dream of Hellenizing the Orient had faded rapidly. Few of the projected

Greek-style public buildings were completed, and even the city center, as finally built, was a compromise, occupying barely half the space originally allotted (Fig. 24). The temples of the last three centuries were all traditionally Eastern buildings dedicated to Oriental divinities, including for good measure a synagogue and a church; and by A.D. 250 the monumental buildings of the agora had been engulfed by the warrenlike structures of an Oriental bazaar (Fig. 25). Except for a thin top-dressing of Roman buildings (barracks, baths, a small open market square), the East had reclaimed its own. On the other hand the street plan had proved as effective as it was simple, and it was in full use right down to the end. Individual city blocks were remodeled as needed and others were pushed out into the open ground, but the overall plan was respected (Fig. 23). This may not have been in detail the city the founders envisaged, but it still worked.

5. THE BEGINNING OF URBANISM IN THE WEST

Greek maritime contacts with the west go well back into the second millenium B.C. To what extent these involved the establishment of seasonal or even permanent trading posts, and whether such contacts were intermittently maintained over the dark centuries when to Homer the lands beyond the Ionian Isles were no more than a setting for marvels half remembered, these are problems to which archaeology has still to give a decisive answer. What is certain is that by the beginning of the eighth century B.C. Greek traders and adventurers were again faring westwards. Along the western coasts of North Africa and in western Sicily and Sardinia they found themselves forestalled by the Phoenician merchants of Lebanon, busy establishing what was to become the powerful commercial empire of historical Carthage; and in Etruria they were faced by a people which, while welcoming foreign craftsmen and traders, was strong enough to exclude competitive settlement. When therefore, about the middle of the eighth century, the Greeks themselves began to establish permanent settlements in the west, it was to the familiar coasts of eastern Sicily and of southern Italy that they naturally turned.

Although there is still a great deal to be learned about these early Greek colonies, there have nevertheless been several important advances in recent years. One can no longer maintain that Greek forms of town planning made their first appearance in the west under the influence of Hippodamos, in the fifth century B.C. Again, although the myth of an originally independent Etruscan tradition of orthogonal town planning, already current in Roman learned circles, had until recently a wide following, few scholars today would be prepared to frame the story in terms of a dialogue between two contrasting orthogonal traditions, one Greek, the other Etruscan or Italic. It has rather to be told in terms of a single, broadly developing historical tradition in which Greeks, Etruscans, Romans, and, presumably, Phoenicians and Carthaginians each had a part to play.

Let us start with the Greeks. What were the Greek colonies in southern Italy and Sicily like? Here air photography and excavation are revealing a clear and remarkably consistent picture of a system of urban planning based on the concept of a few widely spaced longitudinal avenues intersected, ideally but not invariably at right angles, by a far larger number of generally narrower cross streets. Apart from the open spaces reserved for the agora, temples and other public monuments, the whole available space was subdivided into a broadly uniform grid of elongated residential blocks, which might be anything up to eight times as long as they were broad. At Poseidonia (the Roman Paestum), for example, there were three longitudinal avenues and at least thirty-two cross streets in addition to the transverse central band of open ground occupied by the temples, the agora and other public monuments (Figs. 29, 30). Several slight anomalies show that, although this scheme is probably of late-sixth-century date, it is later than the sixth-century temples.[15] In other words, it does not represent the original layout of the Greek settlement, but a rationalization and extension thereof. Nevertheless, the fact that such a rationalization was possible at all is itself an indication of a certain previous disposition towards orderly planning.

We can in fact now see that the plan of fifth-century Poseidonia represents ideas of planning which were already taking concrete shape in the Greek cities of southern Italy and Sicily as early as the seventh century B.C., and which were widely practiced there in the seventh and sixth centuries. Similarly gridded layouts, consisting of broad avenues and narrow cross streets framing elongated rectangular housing blocks, have been identified at Metapontum and Selinus (Fig. 31), both certainly before 500 B.C.; at Akragas (Agrigento), dating from the city's foundation in 580 B.C. (Figs. 32, 33); at Neapolis (Naples) in 446 B.C. (Fig. 39), and at Heraclea in 433–2 (Fig. 36). Other examples, not closely dated but probably from the same general period, have been observed at Caulonia and Locri. All of these appear to follow substantially the same model, except at Selinus (Fig. 31), where the scheme of the acropolis layout was modified to suit the limited space available, with one major and one minor cross avenue intersecting the axial north-south avenue at right angles, and with the housing blocks disposed correspondingly in two different directions. It used to be thought that the resulting cruciform scheme was evidence of Roman influence and date, but both the avenues and the housing blocks have now been shown by excavation to be founded on late-sixth-century structures. What is more, air photography has now revealed similar streets and housing blocks in parts of the outer city which almost certainly were never reoccupied after the city's destruction by the Carthaginians in 409 B.C.

When and in what circumstances did these ideas take formal shape? The key excavation in this respect is that of Megara Hyblaea (Figs. 34, 35). Founded traditionally in 753 and destroyed by the Syracusans about 483, the principal factor dictating the choice of site seems to have been the adjoining belt of potentially fertile coastal plain rather than any conspicuous advantages afforded by the site chosen for the city itself. This was a stretch of open ground overlooking the sea and enclosing a shallow valley, with only a modest harbor and no natural landward defenses. Some Greek colonies were primarily commercial foundations; Zancle (Messina) and Rhegion commanding the Straits of Messina, Massalia (Marseille) and Byzantion are conspicuous examples. Others had, or came to have, a double purpose. But for many, probably most, the main objective at the outset was land, and Megara Hyblaea offers a unique vision of the genesis of one of these small colonial landed settlements.

Figure 34 illustrates the northern part of the town and Figure 35 the center of it—the agora—which occupied a trapezoidal open space at the junction of two differently oriented systems of city blocks. The pottery found everywhere in the deepest levels suggests that most of the area within the walls (which rather unexpectedly are not an original feature) was occupied at a very early stage; but the only actual buildings dating from the eighth century are a number of single-roomed houses, eleven of which have been found in the vicinity of the agora. The formal layout of the streets and city blocks and of the buildings enclosing the agora itself did not take place until the second half of the seventh century, during which the agora was enclosed on three sides by public buildings (temples and stoas), while on the fourth side, where alone it was open towards a street, a block of what had been domestic settlement was gradually taken over by other public buildings. In course of time yet others were inserted to the north and south, adjoining though not directly fronting onto what had become the architectural as well as the political focus of the city's life.

Although the excavators have preferred to emphasize the fact that it took a century and more to establish the formal network of streets and buildings characteristic of the historical Greek *polis*, the site of the agora does in fact appear from the outset to have been reserved as an open space, and there must very early have been something akin to the later street plan, since the early houses all respect the latter and are aligned upon it. When the formal "urbanization" came, it could do so without doing violence to the pre-existing pattern. Pending fresh evidence one can only guess at the elements of the earlier pattern. One very likely factor is the initial distribution of building plots within the city, another the formal survey upon which, as in later Greek colonial ventures, we may assume this distribution to have been based. Such surveys might follow or rationalize existing topographical features, or they might create new features, prominent among both categories being roads. At Megara the scheme has all the air of having been so shaped, with the agora situated at the intersection of the two roads which outside the city limits were its most important links with the surrounding territory—the north-south coast road, here the avenue ('B') which determines the alignments of the area to the west of it, and an east-west avenue ('A') of which the slightly irregular course strongly suggests evolution from a very early track leading up from the coast to the interior. The oblique alignment of the streets to the east of 'B' must reflect some feature still to be explored, possibly an early track up from the harbor.

Thanks to the finds at Megara Hyblaea we now know for certain that a neatly rectilinear, near-orthogonal layout could be applied to a Sicilian Greek colony as early as 650–600 B.C.; and there are indications that the formal layout followed closely the lines established by the original colonists. A similar history would explain the anomalies observed at Poseidonia and at Selinus.[16] The historical limelight is edging unmistakably towards that hitherto somewhat shadowy figure, the surveyor who accompanied these colonies to lay out the walls and to establish the equable allocation of land between the colonists. In later times we know that this allocation comprised a building plot within the town and an area of farmland outside.[17] Hitherto it is only the former for which archaeology has been able to furnish clear presumptive evidence. A recent find, near Metapontum, has now given us unequivocal evidence from the countryside as well.

Figure 38 illustrates the territory immediately inland from Metapontum, where air photography and excavation have revealed extensive remains of two schemes of land division. The eastern scheme covers about 40 square miles and is divided by parallel drainage ditches into 38 long strips; with transverse boundaries delimiting individual lots of about 325 by 205 meters. The earliest associated farms date from about 550 B.C. The western area, similar but slightly later, covers about 35 square miles. The discovery raises many historical problems, but it establishes once and for all that the sixth-century Greeks were already using surveying methods comparable to the centuriation of the Roman land surveyors (see p. 28). Similar finds have been made at Chersonnesos (Fig. 37) and elsewhere in southern Russia.[18]

Campania is chiefly important in the present context because it was here that for a time, until 574 B.C., Greeks and Etruscans lived as close neighbors. Etruscan Capua (see below) was a product of that situation. So was archaic Pompeii, with its rudimentary grid and central forum (Fig. 41). Its subsequent enlargement (Fig. 40), a classic instance of the rationalized incorporation of an existing network of suburban streets and buildings, is unmistakably Greek-inspired. Greek planning traditions long continued to dominate the local scene. Medieval Naples (Fig. 39) still kept the street plan and some of the street names of Greek and Roman Neapolis. But after the fifth century B.C. the center of interest and experiment had moved to central and northern Italy.

In central Italy the Etruscans were long credited with the invention of a system of orthogonal planning that was independent of Greek experience and was itself the principal source of early Roman practice.[19] So long as the available evidence was almost exclusively that of an antiquarian Roman literary tradition the mistake was a pardonable one. Already in Varro's day (first century B.C.) there was evidently some confusion between, on the one hand, Rome's undoubted debt to Etruria in the matter of the religious rituals associated with the founding of cities and the formal quartering of the heavens for purposes of divination and, on the other hand, the orthogonal practices of the surveyors and city planners. But Varro and his contemporaries were recording, and on occasion reconstructing, a past that was already remote. Today, thanks to air photography, here and there supplemented by excavation, we know a great deal more than we did about the older Etruscan cities, and there is nothing whatever to suggest that any of them, great or small, was planned other than in terms of the ritual requirements then prevailing and of topographical convenience. This is confirmed by recent excavation. At Veii the orthogonal layout of the acropolis (the Piazza d'Armi) is superimposed on an earlier, random scheme; and at Acqua Rossa near Viterbo, destroyed about 500 B.C., no trace has yet emerged of any formal overall plan.[20]

The contrast is all the more striking, therefore, when one turns to the highly sophisticated planning of Etruscan Marzabotto, beside the river Reno, near Bologna (Fig. 42). This was a city with three broad east-west—15 meters wide—avenues intersected at right angles by a single north-south avenue and a number of smaller streets to form a grid of elongated rectangular city blocks.[21] At the other end of the Etruscan world air photography has revealed what appears to be a very similar situation at Capua, the major Etruscan stronghold in Campania. It is hard to avoid the conclusion that for the Etruscans, as for the Greeks, orthogonal planning was the product of a colonizing situation, involving the formal establishment of new urban centers; and since the planning formula adopted at Marzabotto, and probably also at Capua, was that already current in the Greek colonies of southern Italy and Sicily by the middle of the seventh century B.C., there seems no reason to question that it was in fact borrowed by the Etruscans from their Greek neighbors. Once established, it took on characteristics of its own: possibly, for example, in its emphasis on the intersection of two equal axes (although, as we have seen, this was by no means so alien to Greek practice as used to be believed); certainly in such matters as drainage and water supply, in which the Etruscans were well ahead of their Greek contemporaries. But it was in essence part of the same broadly developing tradition.

The next steps lay with Rome, at first as a developing community strongly influenced by its more advanced neighbors, both Etruscan and Greek, and then as a rapidly expanding power faced with all the problems of imposing its own forms of urban civilization upon an ever-expanding circle of subject peoples. Most studies of Greek and Roman town planning, faced by the finished products, have naturally tended to emphasize the differences between the two, but at this point one should rather stress the essential resemblances. Both were the creation of peoples to whom the city was the natural political and social unit. Both, after their early, formative stages, were the product of expanding situations involving the creation of many new towns and the occupation and reallocation of their adjoining territories. Both, as a result, were heavily dependent on the activities of surveyors whose store of techniques and training, and whose basic vocabulary of practical expedients, were all in origin Greek. In course of time there were to develop many striking differences, the results of differing local conditions, of differing social requirements, of differing qualities of temperament and taste; but these must all be viewed against the background of a shared historical tradition. The great achievements of Roman town planning were built upon a solid foundation of Greek theoretical and practical experience.

6. TOWN PLANNING IN ROMAN ITALY AND IN THE ROMAN EMPIRE

Archaic Rome had shared with its Etruscan and Italic (Figs. 43, 44) neighbors the early advantages and subsequent disadvantages of an organic, unplanned growth which made the older quarters of the later classical city a byword for all that a city should *not* be. It was not until its emergence in the fourth century as a rapidly expanding political power that Rome was faced, in the new military colonies, with the practical problems of urban planning. The situation was not unlike that which had faced Alexander's successors, but the dimensions both in time and space were very different. Whereas, confronted by the alien civilizations of the ancient East, the Hellenistic conquerors had chosen to establish outright a number of broadly standardized, new, Greek-style foundations, Rome's earliest expansion took place far more slowly and on familiar ground. Many of the early colonies could be planted in existing central Italian cities, where the opportunities for rational planning were minimal; all that was needed was the modernization of their defenses and the redistribution of their land. The military engineer and the land surveyor were from the outset essential features of the Roman planning scene.

At Cosa, founded in 273 B.C. on the Tyrrhenian coast (Fig. 45), the claims of defense were clearly predominant both in the choice of site and in the laying out of the walls; but whereas in the Greek East little or no attempt would have been made to correlate the military and civil elements of a comparable foundation (cf. the near-contemporary Dura, Fig. 22), here, on difficult ground, the architect managed to achieve a remarkably successful integration of the two. At two points, both dictated by the need to provide level ground for the forum, he had to sacrifice the regularity of the dimensions of the street grid, but otherwise the latter is essentially an orthogonal layout of the familiar South Italian type adapted to a Roman situation.

Such street plans were being applied, with varying success, to the hilltop military colonies of central Italy as early as the fourth century B.C., certainly at Alba Fucens in 303, possibly even forty years earlier at Norba, in 342.[22] But in this sort of context—as indeed in Greece at Priene or Knidos—they represent something of a tour de force. It was in the plains that orthogonal planning was more at home, and it is here that we can first detect the influence of the land surveyors, who were already busily at work in the surrounding countryside and who must surely have normally furnished the basic layouts of the new towns also.

The surveyors (*mensores* or *agrimensores*) were a body of professionals, whose work is known to us partly from a collection of surveyors' manuals assembled in late antiquity and partly from the enduring traces of their work in many parts of the Roman Empire. Their training was based on Greek geometry and kindred sciences, and much of their professional equipment was in origin Ionian or Alexandrian Greek. The fundamental instrument was the *groma*, a horizontal cross set on a vertical staff and used for sighting the rectangular grid of *limites,* the balks or paths which constituted the boundaries between each unit of ground and its neighbors. These were ideally, though by no means invariably, oriented, the east-west *limites* being known as *decumani* (sing. *decumanus*), the north-south *limites* as *kardines* (sing. *kardo*). Elongated rectangular schemes were not uncommon, but the normal practice was to lay out squares, which commonly measured 2400 by 2400 Roman feet—the theoretical equivalent of 100 small holdings—and were thus known as "centuries" (*centuriae*). The whole process was known as *limitatio* or *centuratio* ("centuriation") (Figs. 46–48).

Although the centuriation of the territory of a colony was an operation theoretically independent of the laying out of the town itself, town and territory might on occasion conveniently share a common base point (Ammaedara in Tunisia is an example that is recorded by Hyginus and confirmed by the surviving remains),[23] and it was quite common for the main *decumanus* (the *decumanus maximus*) of the survey to be identical with the main east-west street of the town, as in a number of towns along the Via Aemilia in northern Italy (Figs. 54, 63). It is hardly surprising therefore to find a marked tendency for the plans of Roman towns to embody two axial avenues meeting at or near the center; and although the modern convention of referring to these urban axes as *decumanus maximus* and *kardo maximus* lacks classical authority, it does in fact almost certainly reflect the reason for this characteristically Roman development. We find it already operative in the late fourth century at Ostia—the small military colony established to guard the mouth of the Tiber—the strictly rectangular plan of which was neatly divided by two axial streets into four equal quadrants (Figs. 49, 50). (How the latter were originally subdivided we do not know.) Similar plans are known from at least two other early coastal colonies (Minturnae and Pyrgi), a group of foundations which clearly played an important part in the development of a specifically Roman version of orthogonal town planning.

Another early development that can probably be attributed to the influence of the land surveyors is the trend towards square or near-square city blocks. Elongated blocks in the Hellenistic manner did continue to be used, particularly in areas where they were already familiar, and on occasion elsewhere, as outstandingly at Carthage, ca. 35–15 B.C.[24] But the norm of later Roman practice was the square.

Despite the military character of the early Roman colonies, the widespread belief that their plans reflect the contemporary encampments of the Roman armies in the field is certainly mistaken. Frontinus (*Strategemata* IV,1,14) tells us specifically that it was only after overrunning the camp of Pyrrhus in 275 B.C. that the Roman armies began to adopt the sort of formal encampment which, developed and standardized, was to carry them so successfully to the farthest frontiers of the Empire. Once adopted, however, progress was rapid. A century later Polybius (IV,31,10) could already describe the internal dispositions of the camp as resembling those of a city. Moreover, the relationship to town planning soon became reciprocal and continuous. As the legions began to settle into permanent garrison fortresses, the towns must have furnished many architectural models. Sometimes, as in the street plans of Turin (ca. 27 B.C.) and Aosta (25 B.C.) (Figs. 52, 53), the influence was in the other direction, from camp to town; and this must always have been the case in the successive frontier areas, where so many new towns were created and where it was the serving soldier or the veteran who was often the best available source of surveying and building skills.

From the mid third century onwards the center of interest begins to shift away from central Italy. New towns, many of them settlements of veterans, continued to be founded or refounded in the center and in the south right down to the time of

Augustus (27 B.C.–A.D. 14); but here both the setting and the problems were already broadly familiar. It was in the north that Rome, confronted by the almost featureless plains of the Po valley, found herself confronted also with the task of establishing new cities in areas where urban life had as yet only a very precarious hold. It was a new and challenging situation, and it came at a time when many of the characteristic institutions of the later Roman city—the basilicas, the colonnaded piazzas, the theaters and amphitheaters, the baths, the markets and warehouses—were first beginning to take monumental shape. This assuredly was the school where the planners and architects of Roman Spain, Gaul, the Alpine provinces, and Dalmatia learned their craft, and we can only regret that its creators did their work so well. Almost without exception these towns have been continuously occupied ever since. Along the Via Aemilia towns such as Ariminum (Rimini), Caesena (Cesena), Faventia (Faenza), Bononia (Bologna), Mutina (Modena), Regium Lepidum (Reggio Emilia), Parma, Fidentia (Fidenza), and Placentia (Piacenza, Fig. 54); along or north of the river, Ticinum (Pavia, Fig. 55); Cremona, Comum (Como, Figs. 56, 57); Mediolanum (Milan), Brixia (Brescia), Verona (Figs. 58, 59), Patavium (Padova); south of the Apennines Fiorentia (Florence), Luca (Lucca, Figs. 60–62), and Luni, near Carrara; and many others. We know that they were regularly laid out on a formal grid, which in a great many cases has left a permanent imprint on all subsequent growth; we know that many of them were oriented on some part of the road system which they were designed to exploit and control and that they were frequently accompanied by schemes of centuriation (Fig. 63). But with the notable exception of the Capitolium at Brixia,[25] the walls and gates of the public monuments that survive belong to later, more opulent times. We can read the outlines of the first chapter of the story, but for the detail we are almost totally dependent on later evidence, both in Italy and in the provinces.

We have lingered over this early phase because, at any rate in the western provinces of the Empire, the rest of the story of Roman town planning is very largely a matter of the application and elaboration of the models established in the early military colonies. Although after the battle of Actium (31 B.C.) Rome became the undisputed master of the Mediterranean world, it was the size rather than the nature of the problem that was changed. As we have stressed, an axiom of government which the Romans shared with the Greeks was that the natural unit of administration was the city; and since in the west, outside the limited areas of prior Greek or Punic settlement, they were confronted by peoples to whom town life was either unknown or a very recent innovation, a first task in the newly conquered provinces was the creation ex novo of a large number of Mediterranean-type urban centers. Here the lessons learned in Republican Italy served them well. The familiar orthogonal layouts and accompanying building types could be applied to almost any situation. Within a generation, towns on the Italian model were springing up all over the western provinces.

Although in their broad conception these cities personify the Roman liking for standard answers to standard problems, there was nothing mechanical in the way the surveyors and architects went about their task. Terrain, climate, pre-existing roads or urban nuclei—all of these were taken into account. Even where the site was new and the ground almost featureless, strictly four-square settlements such as Thamugadi (Timgad) in Algeria (Figs. 65, 66) were the exception. At Verulamium (St. Albans), laid out very soon after the conquest of southeastern Britain in A.D. 43, the surveyors were quite content to incorporate an oblique stretch of Watling Street, much as the nineteenth-century developers of Manhattan incorporated Broadway (Figs. 67–70). Pre-existing settlements were variously treated. In Gaul, for example, Augustodunum (Autun)[26] illustrates the common tendency to select a new, more convenient site, leaving the earlier, native center to wither quietly away. Other Gallo-Roman towns, such as Lugdunum (Lyon) and Nemausus (Nimes),[27] like many of the originally Punic or Numidian towns of North Africa, incorporated elements or even whole quarters of pre-Roman settlements. Elsewhere, as regularly in the tribal capitals of southeast Britain, the native settlements were in time completely remodeled on Roman lines (Figs. 71, 72).

These new cities were the creations of a self-confident age. Defense played a very small part in the choice of site. Far more important were communications, agricultural wealth, the control of river crossings, natural harbor facilities. Roman London, for example. Like Rome itself, its prosperity was based on the control of the lowest all-weather crossing of a major navigable river; but whereas Rome grew naturally—one might say almost by accident—out of this situation, London was the farsighted choice of some nameless engineer on the staff of the emperor Claudius. Once established, both cities consolidated their positions for many centuries to come by creating a vast radiating network of roads (and in modern times railways).

Once the site had been chosen and surveyed, certain public works were an immediate concern, among them walls and gates, a water supply, a drainage system, and the nucleus of a civic center. Other public buildings could await their turn as the city prospered and grew. It was one of the merits of the standardized orthogonal framework that it lent itself so admirably to piecemeal development over the years. The Old Forum at Lepcis Magna (Fig. 74) started life, probably around 25 B.C., as a reserved open space within what was originally a grid of small, uniform city blocks laid out on the landward side of the old Punic harbor town (which determined the obliquity of the east side). The only building that may be original is the Temple of Liber Pater, the city's patron divinity, followed before A.D. 2 and between 14 and 19, respectively, by the two adjoining temples. Next came the Basilica, and then in A.D. 53–54, pulling the whole scheme together, the square itself was paved and enclosed on three sides with porticoes. The three temples along the southwest side (one of them later a church) were added at intervals between A.D. 72 and A.D. 153, and to this period probably belongs also the Curia, the meeting place of the local council. Finally the forum porticoes and the facades of the two large temples were rebuilt in marble in or soon after the middle of the second century. Thus the development of the city center took nearly two centuries, and yet, like many a medieval Italian piazza, it remained throughout a coherent architectural entity.

A similar combination of sound planning and a stock of familiar architectural types, coupled with the use of local materials and a generally conservative classicizing taste, enabled hundreds of cities all over the western provinces to create, often over long periods of time, their own individual versions of certain broadly uniform schemes of civic architecture. One must not exaggerate. Some of the commonest Roman architectural types (theaters, amphitheaters, and public bath buildings, for example) evolved too late or were too bulky to fit neatly into the pattern. Local architectural traditions, too, had their place, notably in the fields of religion (as in the square Celtic temples of Gaul, Britain [Fig. 72], and the Rhine-land) and of domestic architecture, and again, conspicuously, in building materials and techniques. It was at this level that Roman provincial architecture was best able to express its individuality. Climate and setting apart, nobody could possibly have mistaken Roman Trier (Fig. 64)[28] or Silchester (Fig. 72) for Lepcis Magna (Fig. 73) or Thamugadi (Fig. 65); and yet all four were near-contemporary expressions of the same basic planning tradition. It was precisely in this combination of traditionalism and flexibility that the strength of the Roman system lay.

The type par excellence of the civic center in the western provinces was the forum-basilica complex. Augusta Raurica (Augst, near Basel) was founded as a military colony in 44–43 B.C. As excavated, the forum (Figs. 75–77) was a unitary creation of the second century A.D., but, whether or not it replaced an earlier version on the same general lines, the type was still that evolved in late Republican North Italy: a porticoed, rectangular piazza, closed at one end by a basilica and at the other end framing a temple. In a bewildering variety of closely related (but never identical) forms, this type turns up in early Imperial North Italy at Velleia, near Parma, and at Augusta Bagiennorum (Benevagienna) in Piemonte; on a number of sites in Gaul and Britain, including Lutetia (Paris); in Portugal at Aeminium and at Conimbriga; in Austria at Virunum, the new capital of Noricum, founded about A.D. 45 to replace the old hilltop tribal capital of Magdalensberg; and in Yugoslavia at Iader (Zadar) (Fig. 78) and Aemona (Ljubljana).[29] The builders of the Old Forum at Lepcis Magna (Fig. 74), when they added the basilica, were clearly familiar with the model; and when nearly two hundred years later the emperor Severus ordered a grandiose new civic center at Lepcis it was still to be a hugely monumentalized version of the same general type (Figs. 74a, b).

In the Roman East, with its long-established traditions of urban life, things were very different. Here the impact of Rome involved an altogether more subtle process of assimilation within an existing framework. Understandably it was Roman technology (water supply and drainage, roads and bridges, new building techniques) that paved the way. Among specific architectural types the most successful transplant was the Roman-type bath building, which met a social need and which merged with and eventually came to dominate the old Hellenistic gymnasium.[30] Other western intruders had less success. Many theaters were westernized, but neither the basilica nor the amphitheater ever really caught on.

More important in the long run than any such alien innovations was the development of ideas native to the Greek East. One of these was the scenographic planning tradition so brilliantly exemplified in Hellenistic Pergamon (see p. 18); but whereas at Pergamon this had depended essentially on the architectural exploitation of landscape, there was much in Roman architecture to help liberate this type of urban planning from slavish dependence on its setting. Roman building, with its axiality and artificial vistas and its awareness of the dramatic possibilities of sheer bulk, and above all of the architectural dimension of height, took up a tale of which the prologue to the classical chapter had been written at Halicarnassos, and of which the towering facades of Baalbek and the monumental stairways up to the temples of Zeus and of Artemis at Gerasa (Fig. 26) were the logical sequels. Another facet of the same attitude to the problems of planning was the emergence of such purely scenic types as the great fountain buildings ("nymphaea") of Roman Asia Minor, as at Ephesus, Miletus, Kremna, Aspendos and Side.[31] These were luxuriant stage backdrops, barely skin-deep, built to close a vista or mask an awkward angle.

Closely related to this scenographic trend was the development of the colonnaded street.[32] The earliest recorded example is that which Herod the Great built at Antioch (before 4 B.C.), and while it is tempting to believe that this represented a deliberate monumentalization of the familiar street-side porticoes of late Republican Rome and Ostia (Fig. 50), for the first three centuries of our era the colonnaded street as such was a characteristically and almost exclusively Eastern feature. From a place of passage and a setting for the facade of other monuments, the street became a monumental entity in its own right. It offered a visual unity which was missing in the efficient but rather dull planning of the Seleucids. Used in conjunction with the dominating monumental masses of temples and bath buildings, articulated with arches and crossroad monuments (Gerasa again), and traversed by often similarly colonnaded cross-axes, it became a commonplace of East Roman planning. Antioch, Bostra, Damascus (Fig. 21), Gerasa (Figs. 26, 27), Palmyra, Tyre, Ephesus, Hierapolis, Perge (Fig. 28), Side—it was a poor city that did not have one, and often several. It became as much a status symbol as the arches and monumental gateways of the Roman West. The laboriously terraced, mountain-top colonnaded street of Termessos in Pisidia is a touching monument to such aspirations, reminding us forcibly how much of this civic architecture in far-off places depended on overtones of meaning that are lost on the modern visitor.

7. THE ROMAN TOWN

The underlying theme of this book has been the continuity of urban planning practice throughout classical times. It would, however, be absurd to expect that over a period of a millenium some significant differences did not emerge between the way Greeks and Romans went about things. The element of continuity was rooted in the Greek colonization of Sicily and southern Italy and in the common fund of practical experience gained by architects and surveyors here and later in peninsular Italy. But such experience can be put to very different uses. Viewed in the wider perspectives of human history the Greek invention of a coherent system of urban planning was an epoch-making event. And yet, as between Greeks and Romans, many will feel that the real strength of Greek urban design lay elsewhere, in the sensibility and sureness of touch in the siting of individual buildings in relation to each other, and to their physical setting, which could produce such universally admired masterpieces as Pergamon, Halicarnassos and, in the contemporary orthogonal manner, Rhodes. To a rational-minded people like the Greeks the very logic of orthogonal planning was not without its dangers. A system that lent itself to the sort of intellectual formulation which seems to have been Hippodamos's contribution could all too easily lose its freshness. It was only a short step from Hippodamos to the rather dull, utilitarian formulas of the Hellenistic East.

Roman architects too had their formulas, and they too were all too often content with the sort of drawing-board answers which impose order upon a site rather than seeking to elicit it from the site itself. Nowhere was this truer than in Rome. Fortunately for the historical record, there was no Roman equivalent to the Greek philosophical speculation about the ideal city to confuse the issue (see Appendix 1). The texts record instead, at first or second hand, the practical experience of senior civil servants (Frontinus), working architects and architectural historians (Vitruvius), and surveyors (the "Gromatici"); and because in Republican Italy, and again later in the provinces, Roman planning skills were also the fruit of a continuing grass-roots experience, unfettered by theoretical speculation, the inherited stereotypes of an established tradition of orthogonal planning could be applied with an extraordinary flexibility. Anyone who thinks that Roman provincial planning was efficient but dull need only travel seventy miles from the staid, copybook proprieties of Thamugadi (Figs. 65, 66) to view the breathless, cliff-top improvisations of its sister foundation, Cuicul (Djemila),[33] founded only three years earlier (Figs. 67, 68). Roman planning may not often have achieved the sublime, but it had all the virtues and vitality of a sound, evolving tradition.

With this markedly pragmatic attitude to the problems of planning went a strong concern for the prosaic virtues of material comfort. In most ancient civilizations comfort spelled luxury and was the prerogative of the privileged few. Urban life was the medium by which the Romans contrived to spread an unusually high standard of material well-being surprisingly far down the social scale. Water supply and drainage, public order, the maintenance of streets and public buildings, public entertainment, security for private property—these are a few only of the municipal services available to every citizen. By modern standards there are notable gaps:

education and health, for example. But the list is a long one, and it has left its mark on many forms of urban planning.

Water is the one irreplaceable human need. The classical Greeks had been prepared, where necessary, to pipe it in from some distance,[34] but engineering feats like the aqueduct tunnel of Polykrates of Samos (about 540 B.C.)[35] were exceptional. The average Greek city was content with one or more large public fountains fed by local springs. It was left to the Romans to establish the concept of the aqueduct as an essential amenity of urban life, at first in Rome itself (where the first aqueduct was commissioned in 312 B.C.) but spreading in time to the farthest limits of the Empire. The four aqueducts of Lyon produced some seventeen million gallons of water daily, and one of them was 47 miles long, another 38.[36] The water was delivered to a *castellum divisorium*, a reservoir with settling tanks and a system of sluices and taps to control its distribution to its three principal recipients: the numerous public fountains (which remained the immediate source of supply for the ordinary citizen); the public bath buildings; and the villas and baths of the wealthy private citizen, who was the last to be served but whose rentals were a major source of revenue. Secondary water towers ensured local supply (Fig. 79, at Pompeii). An important by-product was the regular flushing of the street drainage system. Public lavatories (Fig. 80) were normally situated in bath buildings, near fountains, or in other buildings which had a constant water supply. According to the Regional Catalogue, fourth-century Rome had 154 such public lavatories, as against 856 bath buildings, 1,352 water points, 254 bakeries, 290 warehouses, and 46 brothels.

For drainage most classical Greek cities had been, and many remained, content with open gutters. Rhodes, it is true, had a fine system of underground street drains, some of which are believed to date from the city's foundation. But Athens and Olynthus were more characteristic: the slops went out of the window, and any domestic drains simply discharged into the street.[37] In this field the Romans had the benefit of long Etruscan experience (Fig. 81).[38] The first canalization of the stream which became the city's main sewer, the *Cloaca Maxima*, goes back to the sixth century B.C. By the end of the Republic there was already an elaborate network of covered street drains, and similar drainage systems became a regular feature of the laying out of new towns elsewhere. At Ostia the domestic drains discharged directly into the sewers, and in many Italian towns the nucleus of the Roman system was still in use down to quite recent times.

Other refuse was presumably collected by municipal slaves under whatever magistrate was responsible for the care and maintenance of the streets. This was one of the many responsibilities of the *astynonomos* of Hellenistic Pergamon (see p. 16), and in Imperial Rome there were no less than four junior magistrates with this specific duty.[39] How exactly they operated we have little direct evidence; but about a related service, the water supply, we know a great deal, thanks to the survival of the handbook compiled by Sextus Julius Frontinus, who was appointed Water Commissioner in A.D. 97 and who had a large permanent staff of slave workmen and technicians at his disposal (Fig. 82). Rome was a special case, both in the size of its urban problems and the number and complexity of the agencies that dealt with them. But it is a reasonable guess that the basis of such services was everywhere the same—a body of municipal slaves operating under an urban magistrate.

Markets were another essential urban commodity. As a city outgrew the use of the agora or forum as an all-purpose open space, it came to need more specialized buildings, conveniently located. In Rome the cattle market beside the river, the Forum Boarium, may well antedate the Forum Romanum itself.[40] An early specialized type was the *macellum* for foodstuffs, as in the Forum at Pompeii; and for other commodities there were the covered markets, of which Ferentinum (Fig. 43, in the upper city) marks the modest beginnings, and Trajan's Market in Rome and a building at Augusta Raurica (Fig. 75, the "Neben-Forum"), the subsequent development.[41]

Warehouses (*horrea*) for the storage of foodstuffs and other goods are another municipal service that is well represented in the archaeological record, at Ostia (Fig. 83), in Rome (Fig. 84), and in the commercial centers of the provinces, as for example on the harbor moles of Lepcis Magna.[42] Many of them were state owned, under the control of the imperial *Annona* or, in the frontier provinces, of the army. But others were private or municipal property, and wherever commerce was active they were an important feature of the urban scene, dominating the water frontages of cities such as Ostia and Rome itself.

Yet another aspect of Roman daily life which has left its mark on many a later town plan is that of public entertainment. In Rome alone one has the Theater of Pompey, still buried but outlined by medieval streets; the Stadium of Domitian, now the Piazza Navona; the Circus Maximus; and the Colosseum and the Theater of Marcellus, both of which survived as medieval fortresses. Figures 58 and 61 illustrate the amphitheaters of Verona and Luca, of which the former is now once more a setting for spectacles, the latter a marketplace. Such large, intractable buildings tended to be situated on the outskirts of towns but, as we see at Thamugadi (Fig. 66), this was by no means an invariable rule. In any case, wherever situated, they and the great public bath buildings were normal civic amenities, available to the free inhabitants of any substantial Roman town. Taken in conjunction with the generally high standards of Roman housing, they represent a degree of widely shared material comfort and urban sophistication that was without parallel until very recent times.

Once a city was established, what measure of control was there over its subsequent development? A very important factor was undoubtedly the clear demarcation between public and private property. This, as we have seen, goes right back to the foundation of the first Greek colonies, and it was powerfully reinforced by the Roman development of the system of municipal registration to which the Arausio maps (Figs. 47, 48) bear such eloquent witness. Thus, although there are many documents to show that private encroachment on street frontages was an ever-present danger, the successful survival of so many Roman street plans shows that on the whole it was a danger successfully resisted. (Municipal encroachment in the public interest was another matter; to build the Central Baths at Augusta Raurica [Fig. 75] it was found convenient to suppress two existing streets.) There are also scattered references to municipal legislation on such matters as street widths, the maximum heights of buildings (70 feet in Rome under Augustus, reduced to 60 feet by Trajan), and the circulation of traffic. All but certain essential wheeled traffic was excluded from Rome between dawn and dusk, and it is quite common to find access to the forum physically blocked to all but pedestrians.

Such enactments are enough to show official awareness of the problems, and a readiness to act in particular cases. But the most valuable sanction must have been that of municipal self-interest. The acid test was that these cities for the most part were found to work pretty well under the ordinary conditions of Roman provincial life. Not until the barbarian invasions of the third century A.D. did hasty refortification introduce a new and potentially disruptive factor into the equation. Even then in a great many cases (e.g., Comum, Luca, Verona) the claims of defense and of the existing street plans could be made to coincide closely. Where they did not, under the new conditions it was inevitably the defenses which increasingly became the dominant factor.

As for the old, irregular cities—the cities that just grew—the obstacles to radical replanning were many, the opportunities few. One such opportunity was the great fire of Rome in A.D. 64, and by a happy accident we possess Tacitus's account[43] of Nero's regulations for the rebuilding of the city. They embody the best planning experience of the day: regular, wide streets, street-side porticoes, no building more than 70 feet high, wherever possible detached and using fireproof materials. The marble slab illustrated in Figure 84 comes from the huge plan of Rome which was prepared about A.D. 200 for display on the walls of the Library of Peace.[44] It shows an unidentified commercial quarter which lay on the edge of just such an area of orderly redevelopment, the regular streets, tidy rows of shops and warehouses, street-front porticoes, and a bath building (center left) contrasting vividly with the irregular layout below and to the right, which includes (bottom left, on the old, unplanned alignment) a large *horreum*.

Most of the actual remains of domestic and commercial Rome vanished forever in the Middle Ages; and with the example of the Fire of London before us, one may legitimately wonder how widely Nero's New Rome was in fact successful in sweeping aside the entrenched complexities of the old town. But, successful or not, it was a worthy dream; and fortunately for ourselves it was a dream which found tangible and enduring expression in the rebuilding of much of central Ostia over the next eighty years. That the architecture of Rome's harbor town mirrored that of the capital one cannot doubt. Here at Ostia, as in no other city of classical antiquity, one can experience in three dimensions something of the impact of Roman planning skills on everyday life (Fig. 85). It is an experience to savor.

APPENDICES

I. SURVEYOR AND SCIENTIST: PRACTICE AND THEORY
IN GREEK TOWN PLANNING

Thales of Miletus (ca. 624–547 B.C.)—philosopher, statesman and polymath—was universally regarded by later classical writers as the founding father of Greek science. Like most such
traditions, it may be mistaken in detail. Although Euclid believed that Thales invented
geometry, Herodotus, writing in the mid fifth century (II,109), was of the opinion that geometry
may have reached Greece through observation of the land-surveying methods of the Egyptians. As an astronomer Thales' fame rests on the belief that he predicted the solar eclipse of
585 B.C. This tradition too has been contested on the grounds (perfectly correct in
themselves) that Thales' recorded beliefs about the nature of the universe absolutely
precluded any such prediction. But such skepticism is surely excessive in the face of the
evidence, not only of Herodotus (I,74), but also of Thales' near-contemporary and successor,
Theophanes of Colophon. He could well have been using empirical knowledge derived
ultimately from Babylonia, whose astronomers had long been aware of the periodic cycle of
223 lunations, even if they (and a *fortiori* a Greek using their information) could not predict the
geographical incidence of the resulting phenomena.

By the sixth century B.C. there was in fact a large body of observed fact and practical
knowledge already available in the ancient East. The fundamental contribution of the Ionian
Greeks was to make this body of rule-of-thumb wisdom a matter of intellectual, theoretical
speculation. Although the Babylonian astrologer-astronomers had long been observing and
recording the cyclical recurrence of heavenly motions and events, their interest therein was
strictly practical. The calendar, the measurement of time, the orderly procession of the
seasons—these were all necessary tools of the religious system of which they were the
servants. Similarly it was essentially the practical applications of geometry with which the
Egyptians were concerned—for building, or for the surveying of the field boundaries which
were so necessary a part of their system of land registration and taxation. With no more
elaborate instruments than a cord or a cubit rod, some form of water-based leveling device,
and a set square fitted with sights for laying out a right angle (an instrument which can be
constructed by a very simple process of trial and error), they were able to lay out the base of
the Great Pyramid with a linear error of less than 1 in 1,000 and a maximum angular error of 1
in 1,620. They had the empirical skills, but their interest did not extend to the theoretical basis
of such skills.

By converting this inherited body of observed fact and practical know-how into a matter for
theoretical speculation and experiment, the Greek philosopher-scientist laid the foundations
of modern scientific method. They were men of extraordinary intellectual curiosity and
versatility, men whose interests ranged freely across the frontiers of the conventional
disciplines of which they were the inventors and formulators, and who were equally at home
in practical invention and in speculation about the nature of the universe. In the words of
Vitruvius (I,1,16), "men of this type are rare, men such as were, in times past, Aristarchus of
Samos, Philolaus and Archytas of Tarentum, Apollonius of Perga, Eratosthenes of Cyrene,
Archimedes and Scopinas of Syracuse, who left to posterity many mechanical and gnomonic
appliances which they invented and explained on mathematical principles." They did indeed
accelerate beyond all recognition the practical applications of science, but it was above all
the element of pure theoretical speculation which enriched and transformed the intellectual
scene. Within a generation of Thales, his fellow townsman Anixamander had formulated the
notion of a freely floating earth at the center of a spherical universe. Before the century was
out the Pythagoreans had arrived at the spherical nature of the earth itself, followed in the
fifth century by the discovery, by Anaxagoras of Clazomenae, of the true nature of the
eclipses. It only remained for Aristarchus of Samos (ca. 310–230 B.C.) to enunciate the
heliocentric theory of the universe with the earth rotating on its own axis around the
sun—1,900 years before Copernicus.

In geometry the progress was equally rapid, not least because geometry played a vital part
in astronomical speculation. As one might expect, observation continued to outrun rigorous

proof. To quote a single example, Democritus of Abdera (ca. 460–370 B.C.) was the first to state the volume of a cone; but this could not be satisfactorily demonstrated until Eudoxus of Knidos (ca. 408–355 B.C.) had formulated the canonical "method of exhaustion" for measuring and comparing the volumes of curvilinear planes and solid figures. Again, Oenopides of Chios (ca. 500–428 B.C.) was credited by Eudemus, pupil of Aristotle and first historian of mathematics, with having been the first to investigate the problem of Euclid I.12, namely that of dropping a perpendicular from a given point onto a given straight line. What in fact he was investigating was the theoretical justification for a practice familiar to any surveyor or master builder since early Pharaonic times.

The Greek word *geometria* means literally "earth measurement," and Herodotus was surely right in attributing the invention of the science of geometry to observation of the practice of land surveyors. But one would not have had to travel to Egypt for inspiration. As we can now see at Megara Hyblaea and Metapontum, comparable practices were part of the stock-in-trade of the earliest Greek colonists. Miletus was herself the mother city of many colonies.

With this instance before us, it is easier to understand the later classical insistence upon Hippodamos as the "inventor" of town planning. The very success of Greek philosophical speculation and its capacity for articulate expression inevitably focused the historical spotlight upon the theorist at the expense of the anonymous everyday practitioner from whose experience so much of the theory sprang. Hippodamos, formulator as well as theorist, was almost bound to dominate the later historiographical scene.

To the same general climate of ideas belongs the familiar Greek debate about the ideal city. A passage in Aristophanes (*Birds*, 905–1009), which has led to much past misunderstanding, introduces Meton (an astronomer, best known for his reform of the calendar) as a would-be planner for the new city of the birds. Meton's proposed design is circular, divided into four quadrants (*tetragōnos*); the agora is at the center, and from it radiate the roads, "like the rays of a star." Circular or star-shaped plans are a familiar feature of many historical planning systems (e.g., Palmanova [1598] in the Veneto, the Place de l'Etoile in Paris, the Prati district in Rome), but there is not the slightest trace of any such schemes in actual classical usage, which is invariably rectilinear and by preference orthogonal.

Meton's city belongs to the same world of abstract philosophical speculation as Plato's circular city of Atlantis (*Critias* 112 a–e, 115 a–c) or the geometrically perfect ideal city of the *Laws* (705 a–e). In such circumstances it is the terms of the discussion rather than the detailed proposals which reflect contemporary situations. In this particular case the ultimate formal inspiration of the circular city may be Oriental. The Assyrians were certainly building circular walled cities or fortresses in the ninth century B.C., and the tradition was picked up in Parthian and Sasanian Iran (e.g. Hatra and Firuzabad) and again in Mansur's Baghdad. These were all the creations of people who were restless builders of new cities, and they moved in a world of strong astronomical-astrological overtones. In this respect Meton's ideal city and "Roma Quadrata" (see note 19) may share a remote common ancestry.

II. GREEK AND ROMAN FOUNDATION PROCEDURES AND A NOTE ON ORIENTATION

For the Greeks the foundation of a colony (*apoikia*) was essentially a political act, the substance of which was normally set out in a foundation decree. As always in antiquity there were certain religious formalities to be observed. One such was the consultation of an oracle, for preference that of Delphi, regarding the choice of site. Herodotus (V, 42) was voicing an opinion which few Greeks of his day would have contested when he attributed the Libyan misadventures of the Spartan would-be colonist Dorieus to his failure to consult Delphi or "to observe the (other) practices dictated by custom." Again the actual laying-out of the site was regularly preceded by sacrifices and prayers, as described in detail by Pausanias (IV, 27, 5–7) in his account of the foundation of Messene in 370 B.C., or again in the fourth-century inscription regulating the formal enlargement of the city of Kolophon (see p. 17). But such rituals were normal to any major event of public life, an act of prudent insurance against possible supernatural displeasure. They in no way invalidate the assertion that the decision to establish a new colony was a political decision, and that the considerations governing the execution of that decision were of a severely practical nature.

The evidence for the actual foundation procedures of the early Greek colonies is tantalizingly fragmentary, and there was clearly a wide range of choice open to the initial organizers in laying down the detailed arrangements. One consistent feature is that the enterprise was put under the control of a single leader, the *oikistes*, who in the earlier period at any rate seems to have had virtually autocratic powers. Another is that the colonists who accompanied him, in addition to certain specified common rights and obligations, were entitled to equal allocations of land both inside and outside the city walls; witness Thucydides's account (I, 27, 1) of the Corinthian colonization of Epidamnus, or the foundation decree of Cyrene (*Supplementum Epigraphicum Graecum* IX, 3, 27 ff.). Not all of this could take place immediately. Before the outlying lands could be distributed, the colonists had to obtain physical possession of the surrounding countryside; and one of the results of recent work in South Italy and Sicily has been to define the approximate limits of several such territories (e.g., *Atti del VII Convegno di Studi sulla Magna Grecia*, Naples, 1969) and to illustrate, at Metapontum, the actual processes of distribution (see p. 24). From the moment of landing a key member of the enterprise must have been the *horistes* (literally the establisher of boundaries, or *horoi*). In Diodorus's account of the foundation of Thurii (see p. 16) we catch a glimpse of him establishing the line of the city's defenses, delimiting the areas reserved for temples and other public buildings and, as we can now see at Megara Hyblaea, laying out the building plots within the city and establishing the basis of an orderly street system. The appointment of a specific land commissioner (*geōnomos*) was probably a later development, as in the frankly imperialist Athenian colonies (*klēruchies*) of the fifth century B.C. The *horistes* was in essence a man of practical skills and, as we have seen, the founders of Greek theoretical geometry would not have had to look far beyond their own doorsteps for inspiration.

The foundation of a Roman *colonia* too was a political act, and the considerations governing the choice of site and the details of its lay-out were once again essentially of a practical nature. This must be stressed because the Romans were also traditionalists, clinging tenaciously to many of the rituals and taboos which they had inherited from their peasant ancestors. In this, as in almost any other aspect of Roman public life, there were certain proper forms to be observed which one disregarded at one's peril. Thus, for example, the land-surveyor's instrument, the *groma*, had to be planted with all the proper auspices of good omen; or again, when it came to the physical occupation of the town site, it was the founding commissioner's task to mark out the line of the walls and gates by ploughing a symbolic furrow, the *sulcus primigenius*, with a bronze plough yoked to a pair of oxen, male and female, as Romulus was believed to have done, lifting the plough at the places chosen for the gates. One must not underrate the significance of such rituals, which constituted the ultimate sanction for such important aspects of city life as the inviolability of duly established boundaries and the prohibition of burial inside the *pomerium*, i.e., within the formally sanctified area that adjoined the city walls. But it would be a great mistake to imagine that they played any serious part in determining the initial location and lay-out of the new city. If the first colonists of Cosa did indeed succeed in acting out the ritual of the *sulcus primigenius* around the perimeter of their rocky hill-top site, they did so unquestionably on the basis of a plan that had already been determined in detail by considerations that were almost exclusively practical.

The responsibility for the actual establishment of a new colony was normally entrusted to three specially-nominated, high-ranking commissioners, the *tresviri coloniae deducendae*, whose duties included the definition of the boundaries of the new territory and its subdivision into allotments, the enrollment and establishment of the settlers, the drawing-up and publication of a detailed foundation charter (several of which have in part survived), and the appointment of the first holders of public office. For this the commissioners received full discretionary powers (*imperium*) and a staff of which a group of trained surveyors (*agrimensores*) was an all-important element. There might also be assistant land-commissioners (*finitores*, literally "establishers of boundaries") to supervise the work of survey and distribution. The results of their work were formally recorded for public display in the sort of form of which the Arausio official plans (p. 35, figs. 47, 48) give us a precious glimpse.

An aspect of town planning to which both Greek and Roman writers on the subject devote considerable attention is that of the proper orientation of cities; see notably Aristotle, *Politics*, VII.10,1330a; Vitruvius, I,6,1. Here, particularly in Roman planning, one must distinguish carefully between the practical requirements of the surveyor and the religious overtones of the augural rituals which Roman practice imposed upon him. Both the priestly taker of omens, the *augur*, and the surveyor needed to know the points of the compass and might well have gone the same way about determining them (see Vitruvius, I,6,6–7; for a more rough and ready countryman's method, Pliny, *NH*, XVIII, 76–77). It does not follow that they did so for the same reasons. Another practice which the *agrimensor* shared with the *augur* (and may well have derived from him) is that he did not work in terms of north-south and east-west, as such, but of right and left and of forward and backward. The resulting pattern on the ground is the same, but the difference is important when it comes to interpreting documents such as boundary stones and official plans.

Another important distinction is between the laying-out of open countryside and that of the streets and walls of a town. In the countryside the *agrimensor* was advised by the manuals to adopt an orientation conforming to the points of the compass and, all else being equal, he normally did so, although he was neither meticulously precise in his orientation (Dilke's illustration [fig. 65] of the eight centuriation schemes recorded from the Orange-Avignon area shows no less than seven slightly differing alignments), nor did he hesitate to deviate by anything up to 45 degrees if some dominant topographical feature (such as the line of the Via Aemilia in the lower Po valley; Fig. 54) made it convenient to do so. Working in a town, the same man might find it convenient to use the same base line as in the adjoining countryside (as again along the Via Aemilia), but just as commonly he did not. For every city that was precisely oriented there are an half-a-dozen that were not.

The archaeological record emphatically confirms the explicit testimony of classical writers from Aristotle onwards that the criteria followed in establishing the orientation of a new town were primarily topographical and hygienic, not religious. The direction of the prevailing winds figures prominently. Other common factors were slope (facilitating drainage), the passage of a major road, or a sea frontage. At the level of individual buildings care was taken to give a southern exposure to the living rooms of houses, for penetration by, and exclusion of, the sun in winter and summer respectively (see Xenophon, *Memorabilia*, III,8,9). Bath buildings were sited so that the hot rooms faced southwards or south-westwards. Temples on the other hand regularly, though not invariably, faced east. In short, orientation was an important item in the city planner's calculations, but except for religious buildings the reasons once again were severely practical.

For further reading on the establishment procedures of Greek colonies, see: A.J. Graham, *Colony and Mother City in Ancient Greece* (Manchester, 1964); Martin (1964), pp. 38 ff.; R. Uggeri in *Parola del Passato*, XXIV (1969), p. 68. For details on these procedures in Roman colonies, see: Salmon (1969), pp. 19 ff; F. E. Brown, *Cosa 2 (Memoirs of the American Academy in Rome*, XXVI, 1960) 9–19, describing actual traces of foundation rituals. There is a good summary of orientation in Castagnoli (1971), pp. 61–62.

III. THE IMPERIAL FORA OF ROME

The individual monuments of the city of Rome, such as its basilicas and its bath-buildings, were widely admired and copied, but that was virtually the extent of its contribution to the urban planning of the Roman world. Except for the quarters laid out after the great fire of A.D. 64 (p. 36), it was in fact a city which grew without ever achieving a rational plan. The only other areas which may be said to have been developed in any orderly manner were Agrippa's development of the Campus Martius (unfortunately known to us only in very fragmentary form), the Imperial palace on the Palatine, and the Imperial Fora. The last-named took shape one by one over a period of 150 years; but each was to some extent a logical extension of its predecessors, and together they illustrate in microcosm the ebb and flow of ideas which gave Roman urban architecture its own very distinctive flavor (Fig. 86).

The first of the series, the Forum Iulium, was planned by Julius Caesar and carried out by Augustus. Topographically and functionally it was designed to be an extension of the Forum

Romanum, occupying the area immediately behind the Senate House. Though several times restored, the plan remained that of its first builders, a rectangular open space enclosed on three sides by porticoes and, backed up against the narrow north-west end, a temple to the divine ancestress of the Julian family, Venus Genetrix; opening off the south-west side were rows of offices or shops and Rome's first public library. This plan reflects at least three convergent strains. One is that of the Italic forum, flanked by rows of shops. Another is that of the Italic temple facing out over and dominating the open space before it, as for example the Capitolium (soon after 89 B.C.) dominated the forum at Pompeii. The third came from the Hellenistic East, where Caesar had conformed to the long-established local tradition of conferring divine honors on the living ruler and had permitted the establishment of *Kaisareia* at Alexandria and Antioch. These influential buildings are lost, but we know that such buildings were inward-facing, colonnaded enclosures, rectangular (the Ptolemaion at Rhodes [c. 300 B.C.] occupied an entire city block; Diodorus XX, 100, 4) and that in at least one case (the sanctuary of Ptolemy III and Berenice at Hermoupolis Magna, c. 240 B.C.) they were symmetrically disposed about the longer axis, from entrance to temple. Rome itself was not yet ready for the explicit introduction of the cult of the living ruler. The temple of Venus was an acceptable compromise and the tightly-enclosed, inward-looking precinct a clear echo of the eastern models.

The second and fourth members of the series, the Forum Augustum (2 B.C.) and the Forum Transitorium (A.D. 97) followed essentially the same design, dominated respectively by the temples of Mars the Avenger and of Minerva, the Augustan building being further enriched by a pair of semicircular courtyards set behind the flanking colonnades, while the Forum Transitorium was little more than a long, narrow, space-filling monumentalization of the access road to the Forum Romanum from the crowded slums of the Subura. The third, Vespasian's Temple of Peace (Templum or Aedes Pacis; A.D. 75) was, as its name implies, the odd-man-out of the series, less a place of public business than (in modern terminology) an arts center. The distinction was reflected in its plan, a porticoed enclosure wider than it was long and laid out as a formal garden, and a rather modest temple building, axial to but on the same scale as the row of libraries, museum halls and lecture rooms with which it shared a common frontage. Architecturally this was a reversion to the Italo-Hellenistic traditions of Campania, positively reticent by Roman standards and remarkable chiefly for the richness of its materials and the artistic wealth of its contents (paintings and sculptures by famous Greek artists, the spoils of the Temple of Jerusalem). In one of the halls was later displayed the Severan map of Rome (p. 36).

In one respect the Forum of Trajan (A.D. 113), the fifth and last of the Imperial Fora, neatly rounded out the series by a grandiose restatement of the basic theme of the Forum Augustum, with its confronted, flanking hemicycles; but it also broke with precedent by substituting for the axial Temple a huge transverse basilical hall, the Basilica Ulpia. Beyond this a pair of small, galleried courtyards enclosed Trajan's Column, and beyond this again, on axis and added by his successor, Hadrian, rose the bulk of the temple of the Deified Trajan. Forum and basilica were both long-established and characteristically Roman building types, but this was the first time that they had been used in Rome as the components of a single planned architectural scheme. This is a remarkable fact when one reflects that elsewhere they had long merged into one of the standard planning formulae of the urban architect. As we have seen above (p. 31), the forum-basilica complex was almost certainly one of the planning patterns evolved in the Republican colonies of North Italy, whence it had already spread all over the western provinces. In this respect, then, Trajan's Forum was not only the last of the series but also a first resounding affirmation in the capital of the architecture of the provinces. It was an instant success, enormously admired and widely imitated, a notable example of such imitation being the new civic center of Lepcis Magna (Fig. 74a,b). More than any other single building it was probably the Basilica Ulpia which influenced Constantine's choice of the basilica as the standard place of worship for the newly-enfranchised Christian religion.

In terms of planning one may select for emphasis three characteristics of the Imperial Fora, three characteristics which are in reality different aspects of a single attitude of mind. One is their enclosed, self-contained character; though linked successively together as parts of a larger complex, each was in itself an independent architectural entity. Another is their arrogant disregard of their physical setting. Where the architect of Halicarnassos or Pergamon strove to interpret architecturally the natural configuration of his site, and where the Greek-trained architect of Severan Lepcis Magna accepted unquestioningly the framework of an irregular site, exercising all his ingenuity to draw order, symmetry, and balance therefrom, his Roman counterpart acknowledged no such restraints. The great screen wall across the back of the Forum Augustum was an impenetrable barrier, visual as well as physical, between it and the crowded slums of the Subura beyond. Trajan's architect, Apollodorus, went one further. The Column marks the height of the saddle of high ground which he had had to quarry away in order to achieve a level site. The adjoining market buildings show that he was far from insensitive to the possibilities of landscaping. But all his training was to impose himself upon the ground, not to adapt himself to it.

Thirdly and finally we may note what von Blanckenhagen has so aptly termed the "drawing-board mentality" of these builders. The axiality of the plan of Trajan's Forum—the monumental propylon, the great equestrian statue in mid-Forum, the central door of the Basilica, the Column, the temple—all of this was overwhelmingly present in the mind, but it could never have been experienced visually. At one point it was even deliberately masked by the absence of a central door in the rear wall of the Basilica. Nor can it be an accident that, give or take a few feet, this same axis prolongs that of Vespasian's Templum Pacis. There was indeed a unity of conception bringing together the whole complex, but it was a unity of the mind, not of the eye.

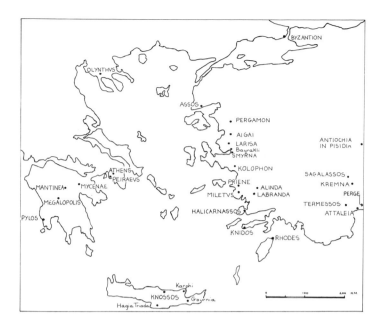

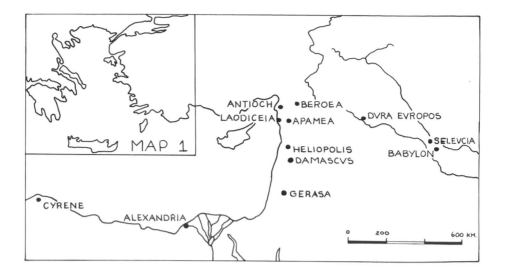

MAP 1

ANTIOCH
LAODICEIA
BEROEA
APAMEA
DVRA EVROPOS
HELIOPOLIS
DAMASCVS
BABYLON
SELEVCIA
GERASA
CYRENE
ALEXANDRIA

0   200   600 KM.

VERVLAMIVM
CALLEVA
LONDINIVM
AVGVSTA TREVERORVM
LVTETIA
AVGVSTODVNVM
AVGVSTA RAVRICA
LVGDVNVM
MAP 2
ARAVSIO
MASSALIA
THAMVGADI
AMMAEDARA
LEPCIS MAGNA

0   200   600 KM.

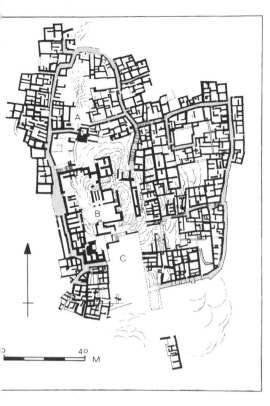

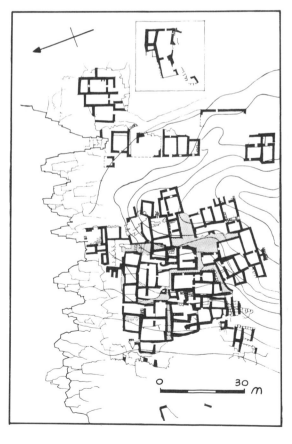

1. Minoan village of Gournia, East Crete. Mid second millenium B.C. A, shrine; B, palace; C, public court.

2. Post-Minoan cliff-top village of Karphi, East Crete. End of second millenium B.C.

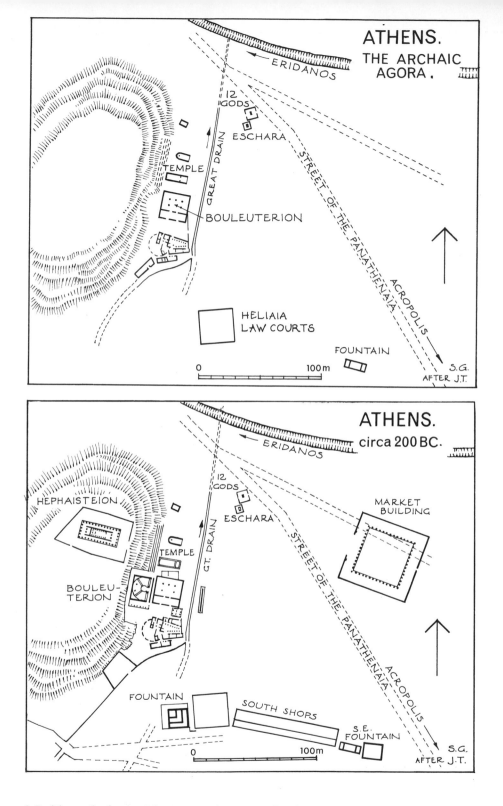

3–5. Athens, the Agora, at three successive stages of its development, from an irregular open space with some public buildings along the west side into a formal enclosure surrounded by public buildings.

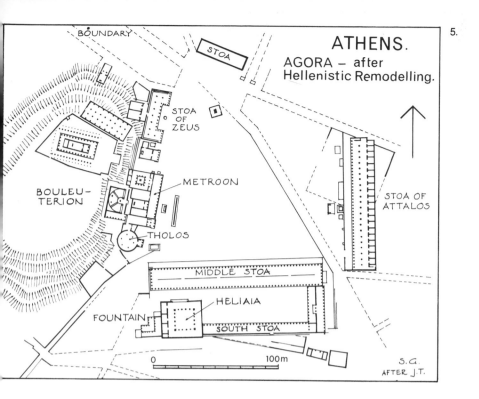

5.

ATHENS.
AGORA – after
Hellenistic Remodelling.

BOUNDARY

STOA

STOA
OF
ZEUS

METROON

BOULEU-
TERION

THOLOS

STOA OF
ATTALOS

MIDDLE STOA

HELIAIA

FOUNTAIN

SOUTH STOA

0   100m

S. G.
AFTER J.T.

. Athens, the Stoa of Attalos (159–138 B.C.).

MILET

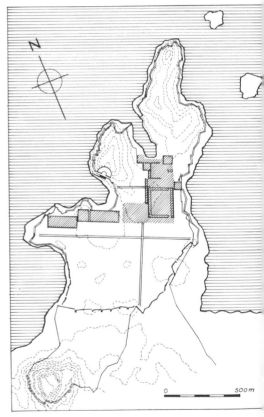

7. Miletus. Layout of the fifth-century city, the walls of
   which at first incorporated an independent acropolis
   (bottom left), but were later shortened and
   strengthened, about 200 B.C.

8. Miletus. Schematic plan showing the main avenues
   and (shaded) the areas reserved for public use.

9. Miletus. Two stages (about 300 B.C. and 150 B.C.) of the development of the public buildings south of the Lion Harbor.

10. Miletus. Restored view of part of Figure 9 (seen from northeast).

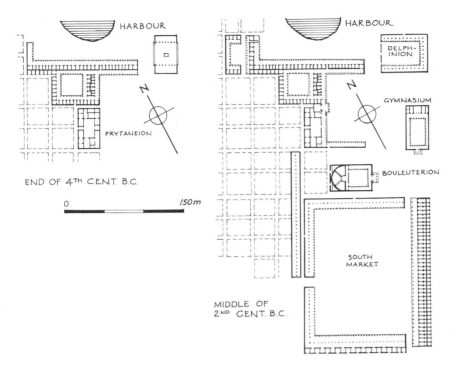

HARBOUR

PRYTANEION

END OF 4TH CENT. B.C.

0   150m

HARBOUR

DELPH-INION

GYMNASIUM

BOULEUTERION

SOUTH MARKET

MIDDLE OF 2ND CENT. B.C.

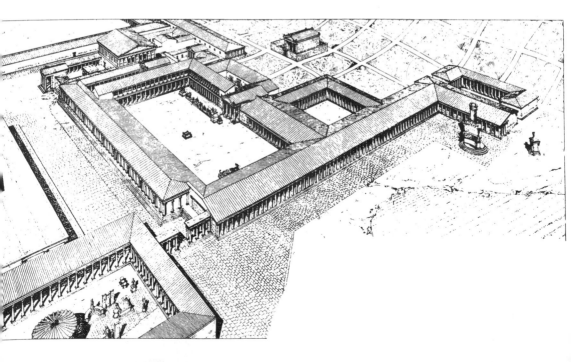

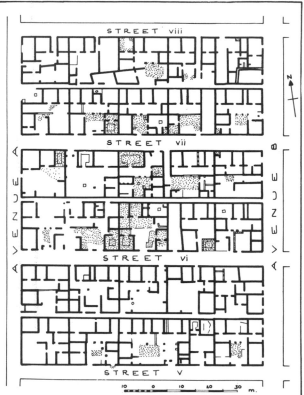

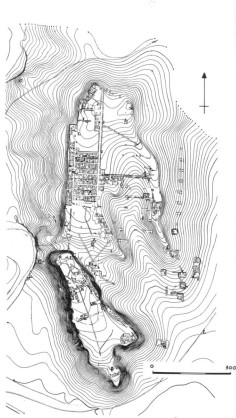

11. Olynthus. Housing blocks of the new city, laid
     out about 432 B.C. (northern section of fig. 11a).

11a. Olynthus. General plan.

12. Priene. Founded in the mid fourth century B.C.

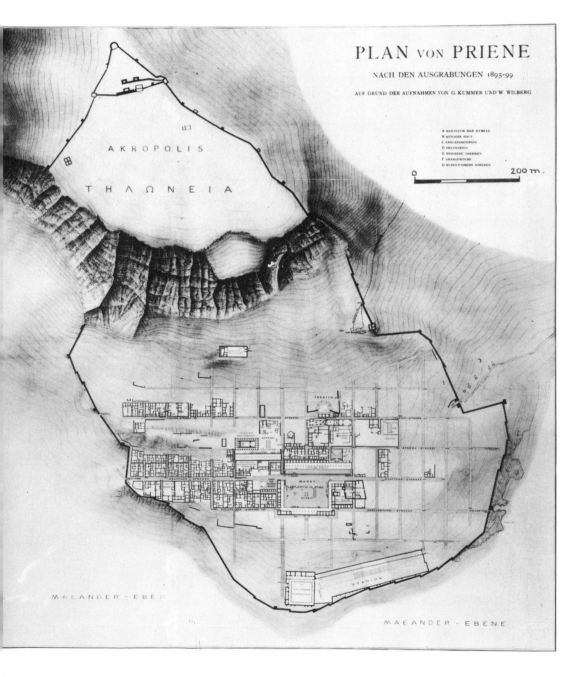

PLAN von PRIENE

NACH DEN AUSGRABUNGEN 1895-99

AUF GRUND DER AUFNAHMEN VON G. KUMMER UND W. WILBERG

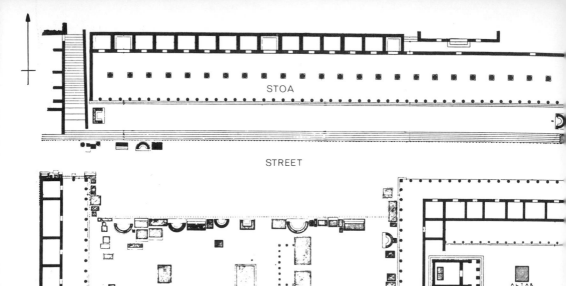

STOA

STREET

ALTAR

TEMPLE OF ZEUS

ALTAR

0   20
M

12a. Priene. Detailed plan of the agora.

12b. Priene. Restored view of the northwest
     corner of the agora.

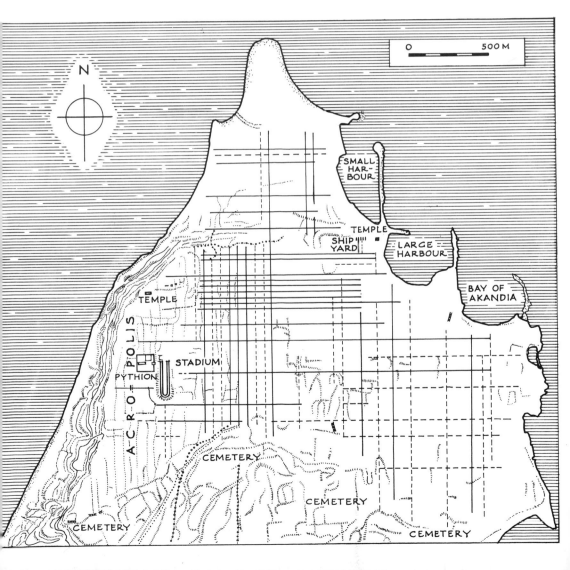

N

0   500 M

SMALL HARBOUR

TEMPLE

SHIP YARD

LARGE HARBOUR

TEMPLE

BAY OF AKANDIA

A C R O P O L I S

STADIUM

PYTHION

CEMETERY

CEMETERY

CEMETERY

CEMETERY

14–15. Pergamon. Plan and restored view of the upper city.
1. Arsenal; 2, Temple of Trajan; 3, Temple of Athena; 4,
Great Altar; 5, Upper Market. Second century B.C. except for
the Temple of Trajan (early second century A.D.).

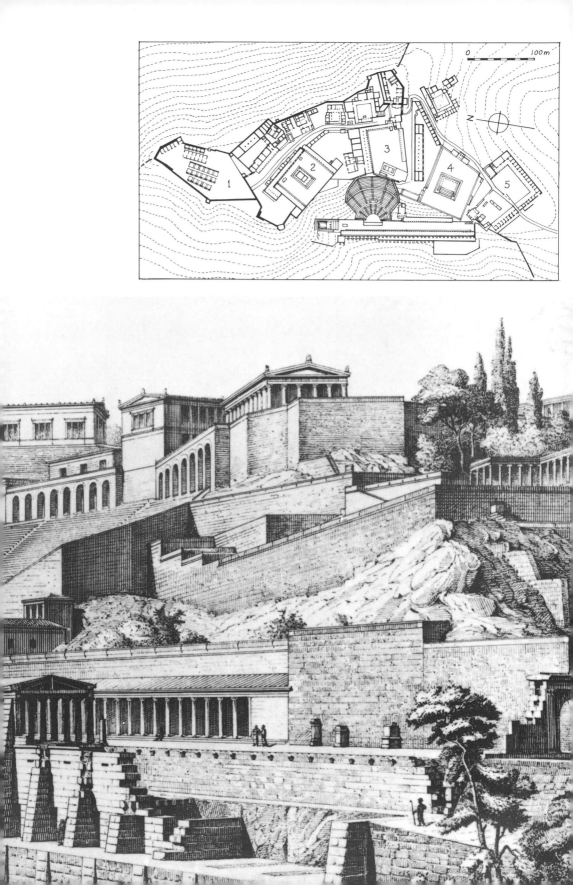

16. Aigai. The primitive hilltop nucleus (above, right) was enlarged in the early second century B.C. on a terraced plan, reminiscent of Pergamon.

17. Aigai. The western part of the two middle terraces, with two large temples overlooking the theater complex.

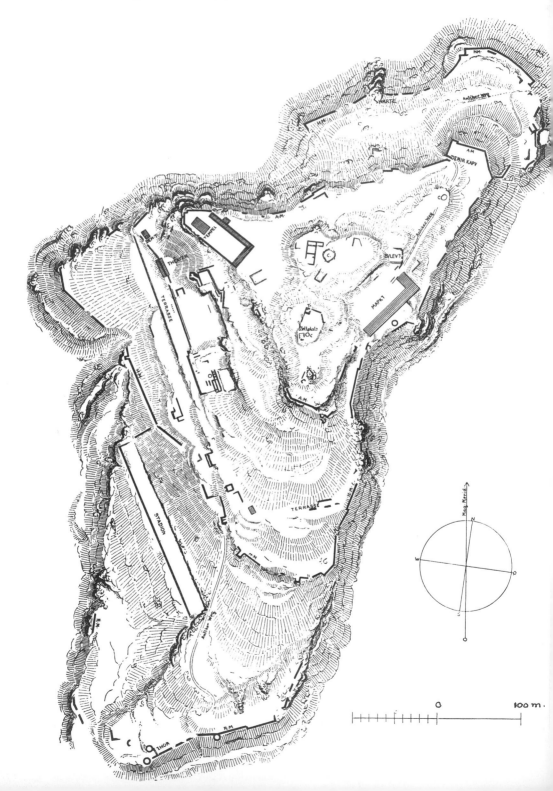

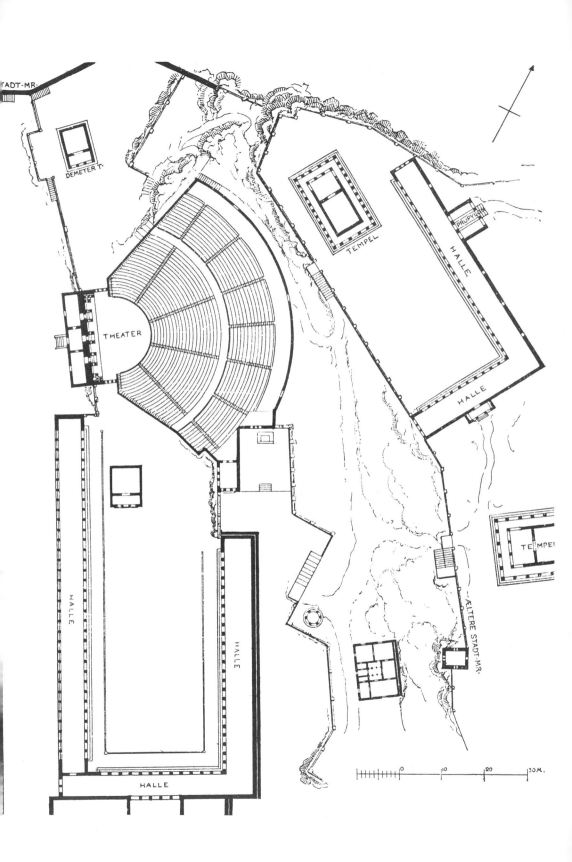

STADT·MR·

DEMETER T.

TEMPEL

PRŎPYLÄ·

HALLE

THEATER

HALLE

HALLE

HALLE

TEMPEL

ÄLTERE STADT·MR·

0   10   20   30 M.

18–19. Assos. Restored view and plan of
the steeply terraced agora.

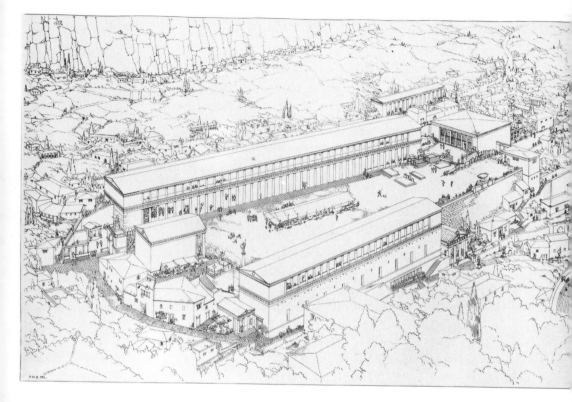

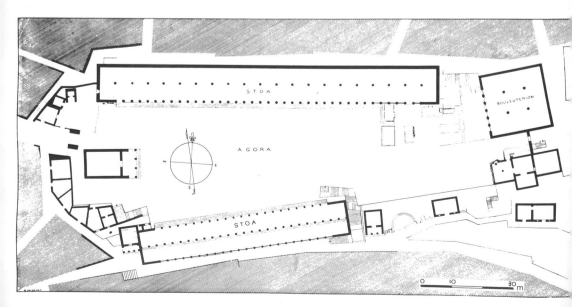

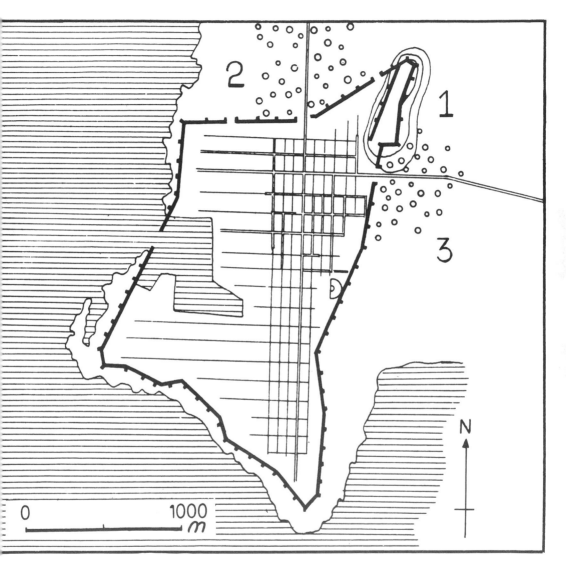

20. Laodiceia (Syria) founded about 270 B.C. 1, the acropolis; 2,3, cemeteries.

0 ⊢———————⊢ 1000
m

N ↑

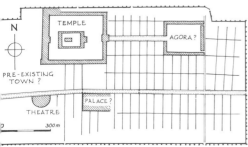

N

TEMPLE

AGORA ?

PRE-EXISTING TOWN ?

PALACE ?

THEATRE

0 ⊢——— 300 m

21. Damascus. The enlargement of the pre-existing town probably dates from the second century B.C.

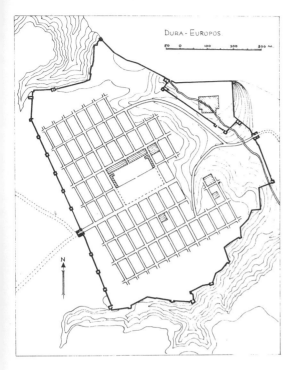

DURA - EUROPOS

22. Dura-Europos (Syria, on the Euphrates). The original layout, about 300 B.C.

23. Dura-Europos. Plan of the city at the moment of its destruction, shortly after A.D. 250.

24. Dura-Europos. The Hellenistic agora, as built. The original plan allowed for an agora twice the size.

25. Dura-Europos. The bazaar quarter, which by A.D. 250 had grown up on the site of the Hellenistic agora.

DURA - EUROPOS

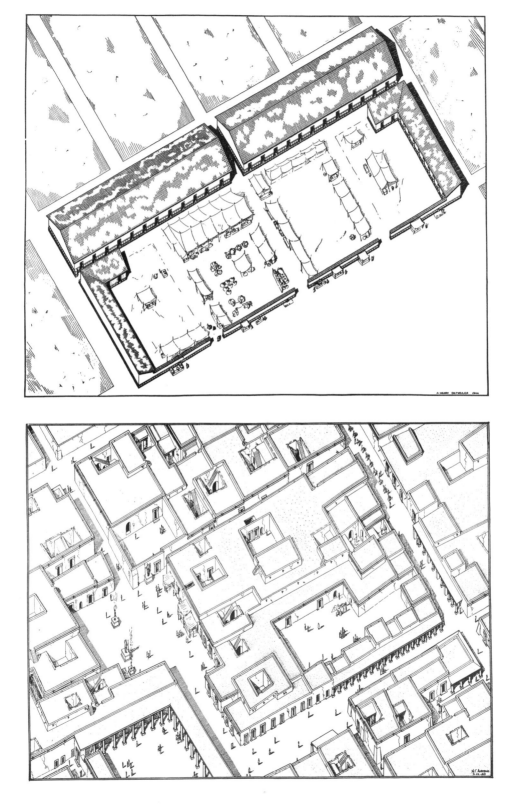

26. Gerasa (Jordania, south of Damascus). As it stands, a Roman creation of the first two centuries A.D. The Hellenistic town occupied the hill at the south end, occupied later by the south theater.

27. Gerasa. The oval "forum" (a caravan market) and one of the colonnaded streets.

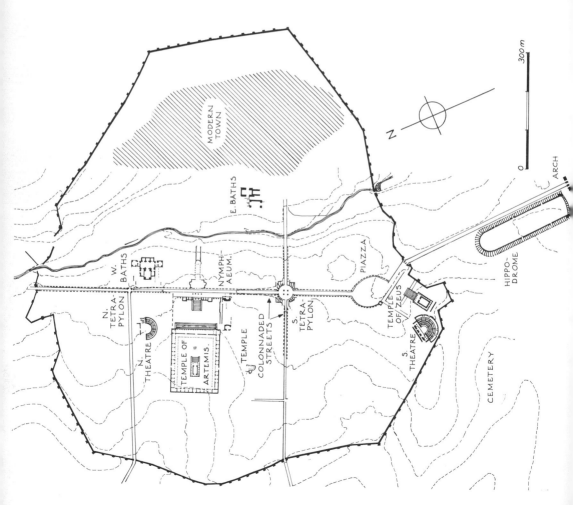

28. Perge (Pamphylia). Colonnaded street with a central water channel, looking southwards towards the inner courtyard of the South Gate.

29–30. Poseidonia (Paestum). The street plan (probably late sixth century B.C.) is clearly visible at many points on the air photograph. The walls are probably of the fourth century B.C.

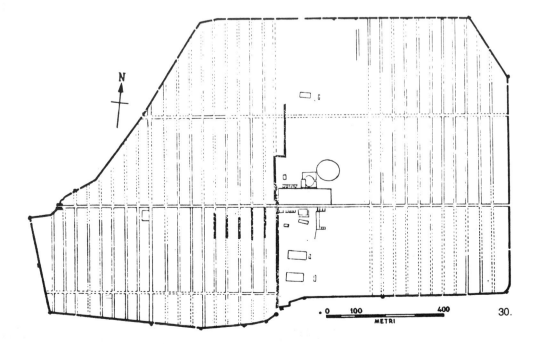

N

0   100   400
METRI

30.

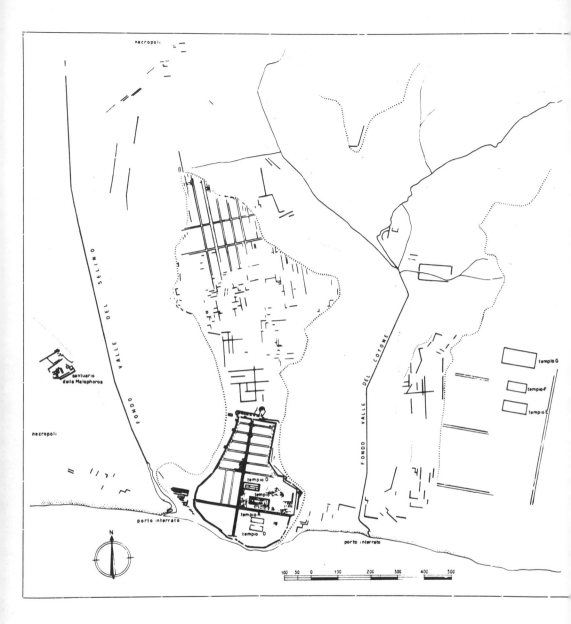

31. Selinus (Sicily). The visible remains within the acropolis date
from the fourth century B.C. refoundation, but they conform to a
much older (sixth century) layout. The grid of streets to the north,
known from air photographs, antedates the city's destruction in
409 B.C.

32. Akragas (Agrigento, Sicily). Founded 580 B.C. Much of the street layout may be of sixth century date.

33. Akragas. Excavated quarter, as of late second century B.C., but following the lines of the original layout.

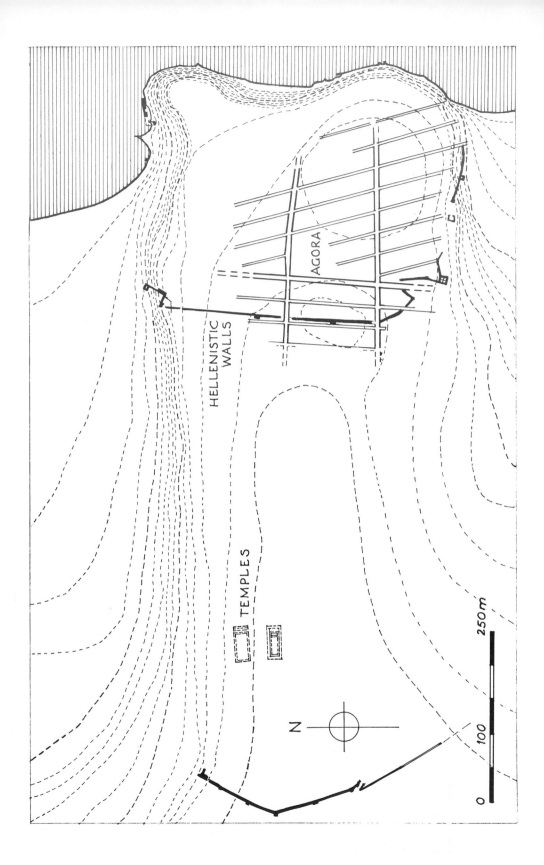

TEMPLES

HELLENISTIC
WALLS

AGORA

N

0   100   250m

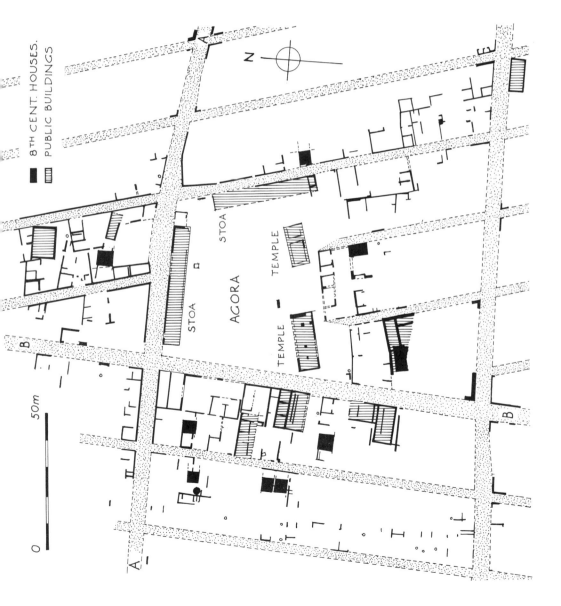

■ 8TH CENT. HOUSES.

▥ PUBLIC BUILDINGS

50m

0

N

A

B

A

B

STOA

STOA

AGORA

TEMPLE

TEMPLE

34. Megara Hyblaea (Sicily).
About 750 B.C.–483 B.C. The
northern part of the site showing
(right) the excavated city center and
(left) two large temples and the city
walls.

35. Megara Hyblaea. The developed plan
of the agora and adjoining streets,
shown in relation to the houses of
the original settlement.

36. Heraclea (Policoro, Gulf of Taranto). Founded 432 B.C. The agora occupied the west end, the acropolis the east end, of the narrow northern ridge.

37. Chersonesos, near Sevastopol (Crimea). The subdivisions of the territory of the Greek colony (c. 420 B.C.) on the peninsula of Majacij. 1, Salt Lake. 2, Cossack Bay. 3, 4, 6, 7, 9, Farms. 5, 10, Chalk kilns. 8, Quarry

38. Formal layout of the territories of Metapontum (right and center) and of Heraclea (left). The dotted line is that of the coast in classical times.

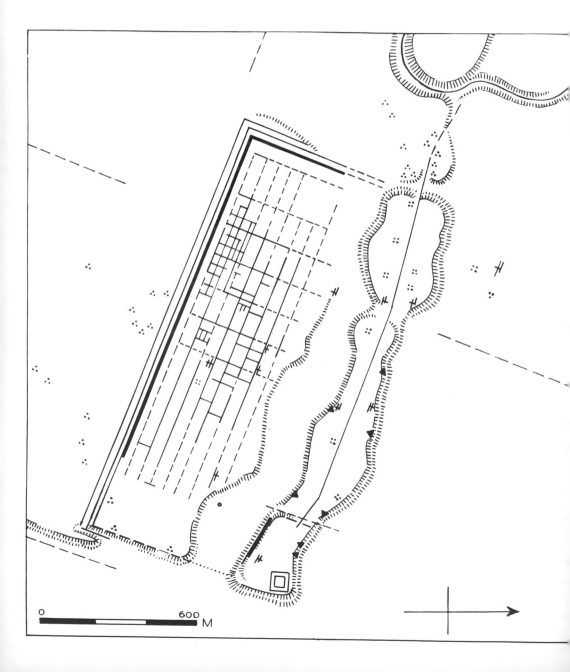

Казачья бухта

① Солёное оз

② Казачья бухта

⑩ К Извес печь

Ч Е Р Н О Е   М О Р Е

К

⑨ Хут. Красинскаго

⑧ Каменоломня

⑦ Хут. Вяземскои

⑥ Хут. Михаили

⑤ Извест печь

④ Хут. Ухтомскаго

③ Хут. Губера-Аметистова

0   500   1000 m

Per Pomárico, Miglionico

Per l'alto Bradano

0   5 km

Avenia

Bernalda

La Canala

Salice

S. Angelo Vecchio

Girifalco

Feroleto

Andriace

Cerulli

S. Biagio

Incoronata

S. Salvatore

S. Nicola

Termilito

S. Teodoro Vecchio

Pirazzeto

STRADA PREISTORICA

Per il Ponte del Re

Per Taranto

Recoleta

S. Basilio

Petrulla

Tavole Palatine

Per Papatonno

TERACLEA

Scanzano

ACIRIS

CHALANDRUM

Antica   linea   di   costa

CASUENTUS

METAPONTUM

Porto

BRADANUS

z

39. Neapolis (Naples). The broad N–S street (Via del Duomo) is a modern widening of an ancient street. The main E–W avenues ran at right angles to it.

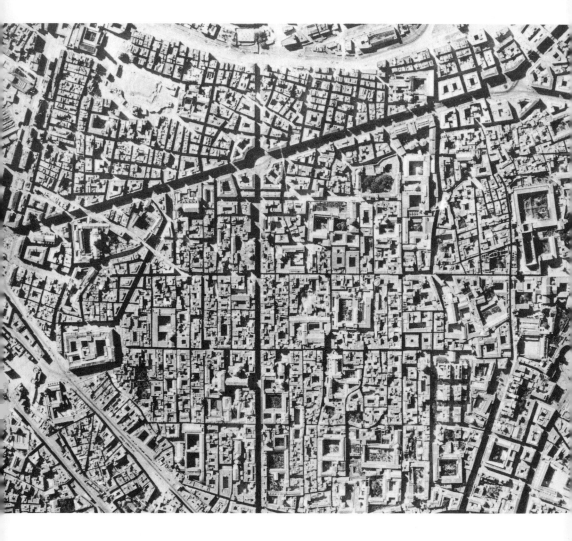

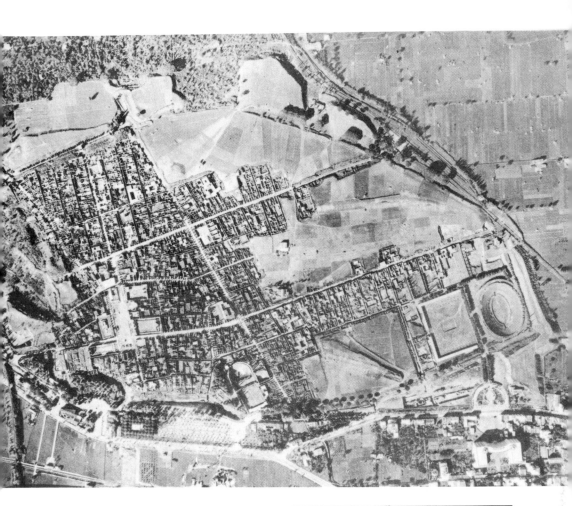

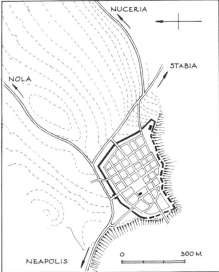

40–41. Pompeii. Air photograph of the city,
destroyed in A.D. 79, and plan showing the
original sixth-century B.C. nucleus and the
network of country roads which determined
the lines of the town's later development.

42. Marzabotto, near Bologna. An Etruscan foundation, about 500 B.C., destroyed little more than a century later.

43–44. Ferentinum (Central Italy). The plan was determined almost entirely by the configuration of a naturally defensible site. The city walls are of the fourth century B.C. and later.

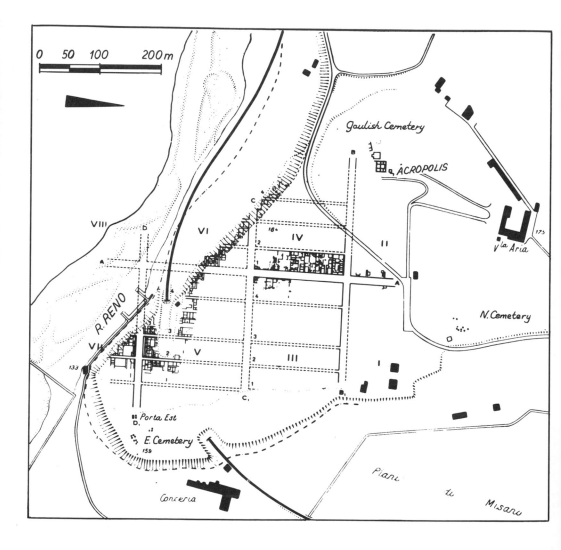

0   50   100   200 m

Gaulish Cemetery

ACROPOLIS

V'la Aria

VIII   VI   IV

II

N. Cemetery

R. RENO

VII   V   III

133

Porta Est

E. Cemetery

Conceria

Piani

di

Misano

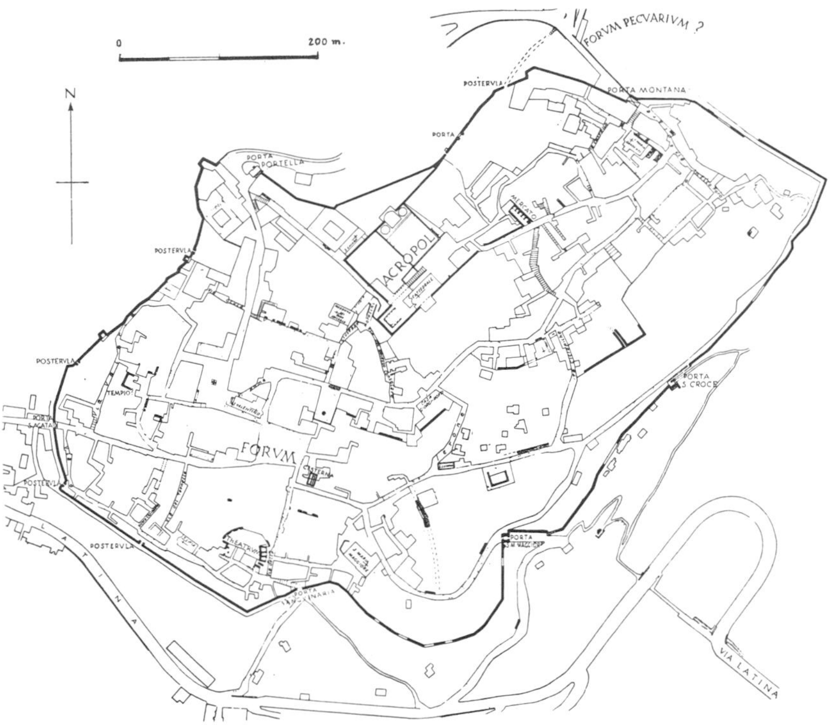
0
200 m.
N
FORVM PECVARIVM ?
POSTERVLA
PORTA MONTANA
PORTA
PORTA PORTELLA
ACROPOLI
MERCATO
POSTERVLA
POSTERVLA
TEMPIO
PORTA S.AGATA
FORVM
CISTERNA
POSTERVLA
THEATRVM
POSTERVLA
PORTA LANCINARIA
PORTA S.M.MAGGIORE
PORTA S.CROCE
LATINA
VIA LATINA

44.

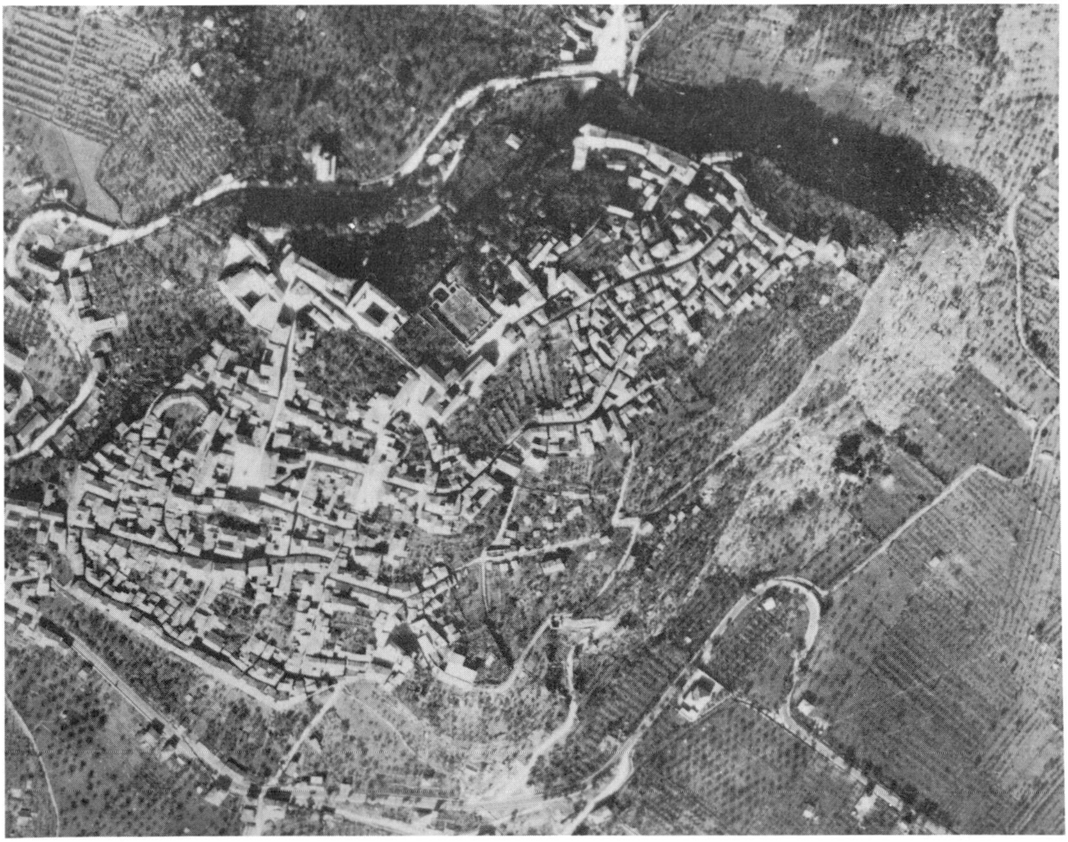

45. Cosa (Ansedonia). Roman military colony founded in 273 B.C. on a rocky hilltop overlooking the sea.

46. Roman centuriation, probably of the second century B.C., the pattern of which is still preserved in the fields of the Po valley plain near Forum Cornelii (Imola).

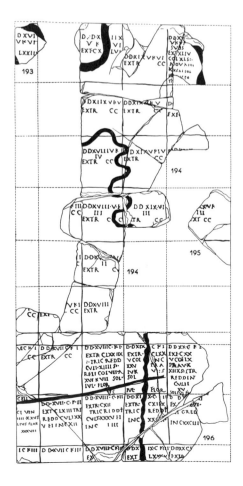

47. Part of a marble panel from an official plan recording the centuriated subdivisions of part of the territory of Arausio (Orange) in Provence. About A.D. 100.

48. Reconstructed drawing of the whole of the same panel.

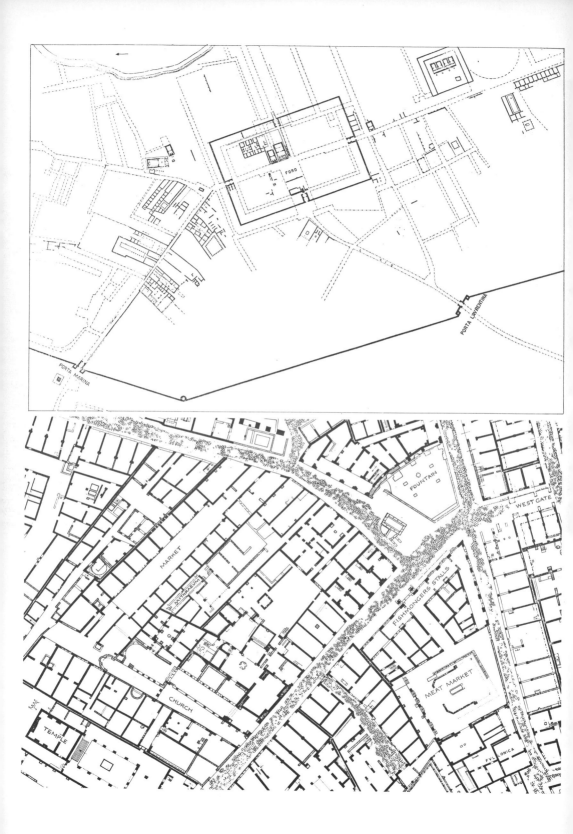

FORO

PORTA LAVRENTINA

PORTA MARINA

FOUNTAIN

WEST GATE

MARKET

MITHRAEUM

FISHMONGERS STALLS

MEAT MARKET

CHURCH

TEMPLE

FVLLONICA

49. Ostia. In the center the military colony of the late fourth century B.C. and, around it, what is known of the unplanned development of the town during the next three centuries. The outer defenses are of the early first century B.C.

50. Ostia. Quarter outside the west gate of the original colony, the result of unplanned growth along two roads leading from the gate.

51. Ostia. Air photograph.

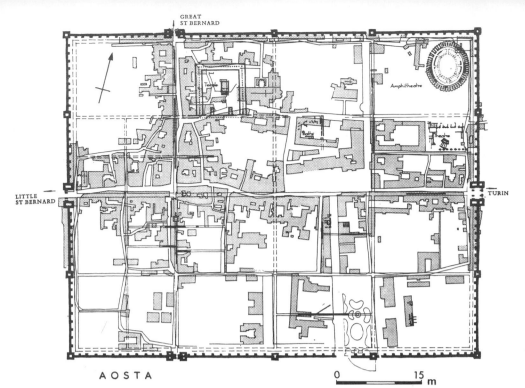

GREAT
ST BERNARD

Amphitheatre

Theatre

LITTLE
ST BERNARD

TURIN

AOSTA

0   15 m

53.

52–53. Augusta Praetoria (Aosta). Roman military colony founded in 25 B.C. The original layout, which is still clearly reflected in the arrangement of the present-day town, appears to reflect contemporary military planning.

54. Placentia (Piacenza). Roman military colony, founded in 215 B.C. The rectangular grid of the Roman town is clearly visible in the center, surrounded in turn by later development and by the sixteenth-century defenses.

55. Ticinum (Pavia). For a time the capital of the Lombard Duchy of North Italy, it has preserved almost intact the street grid of the Roman town.

56–57. Comum (Como). Another well-preserved Roman plan dating from the first century B.C.

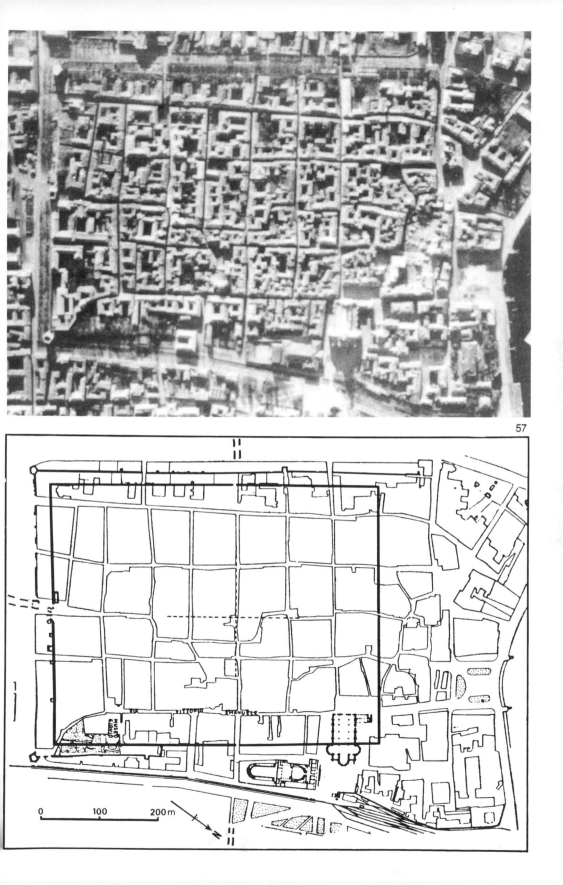

57

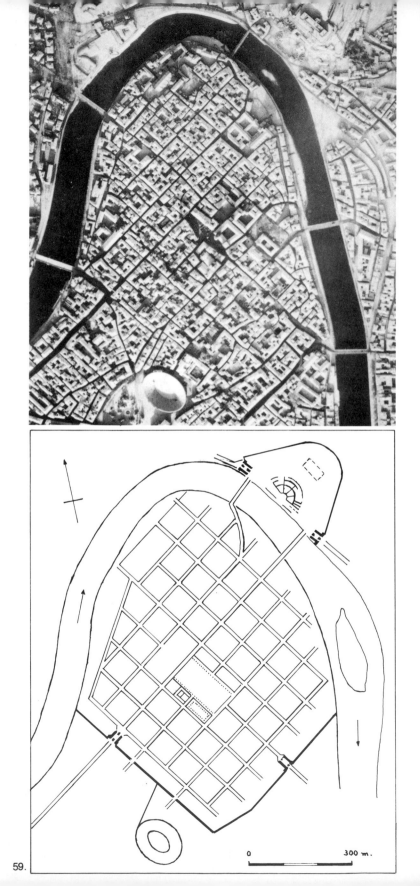

59.

58–59. Verona. Refounded on level ground, probably in the late first century B.C. The earlier town may have occupied the hill on the north bank of the river.

60–62. Luca(Lucca). A notable example of a Roman gridded street layout, preserved through the Middle Ages and enclosed within a sixteenth-century defensive circuit.

60.

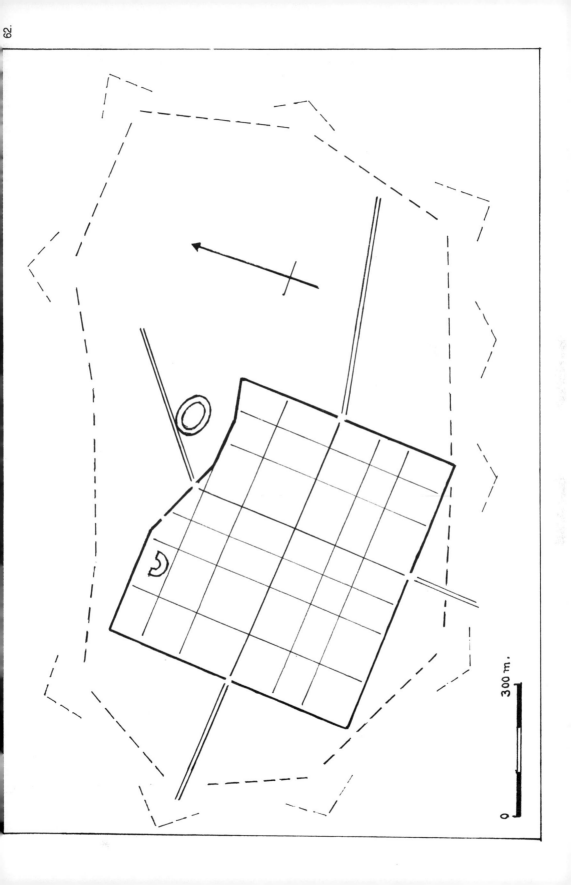

300 m.

0

63. Forum Livi (Forli). Roman market town which grew up, without formal planning, at the point where several roads converged upon the line of the Via Aemilia.

64. Augusta Treverorum (Trier). The bridge and street plan are of the first century A.D., the walls and most of the major monuments of the late third and fourth centuries.

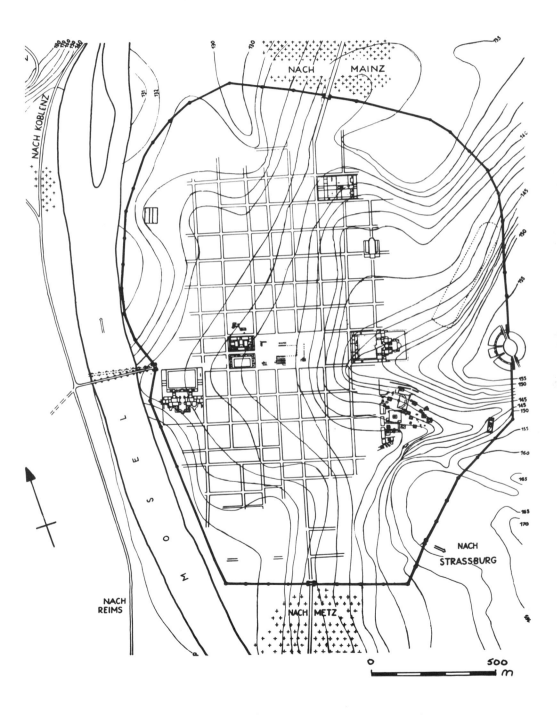

NACH MAINZ

NACH KOBLENZ

MOSELLE

NACH REIMS

NACH METZ

NACH STRASSBURG

0   500
m

65–66. Thamugadi (Timgad, Algeria). The irregular, unplanned growth of the second century A.D. contrasts vividly with the rigidly gridded layout of the original veterans colony (A.D. 100).

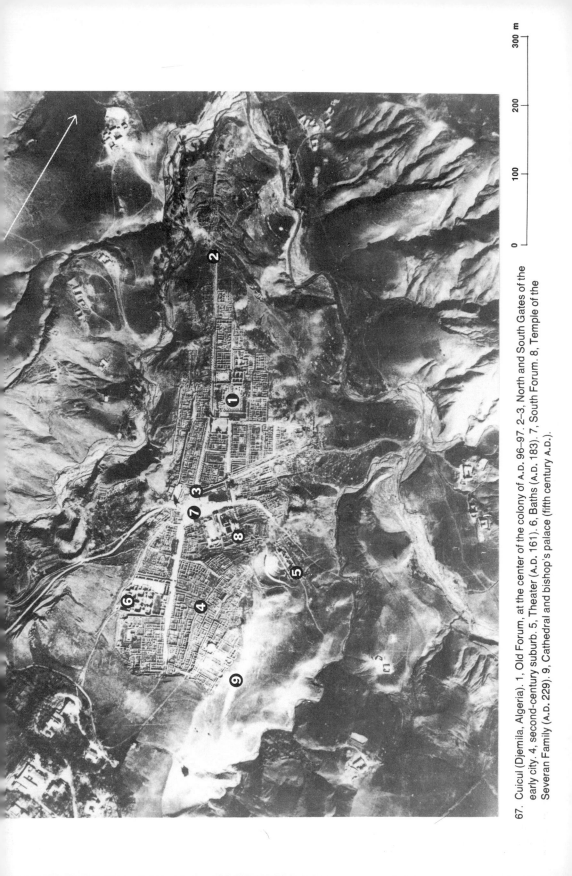

67. Cuicul (Djemila, Algeria). 1, Old Forum, at the center of the colony of A.D. 96–97. 2–3, North and South Gates of the early city. 4, second-century suburb. 5, Theater (A.D. 161). 6, Baths (A.D. 183). 7, South Forum. 8, Temple of the Severan Family (A.D. 229). 9, Cathedral and bishop's palace (fifth century A.D.).

68. Cuicul (Djemila). Temple of the Severan Family (A.D. 229), viewed from the head of the South Forum, which grew up as an open space outside the South Gate of the colony. The arch (bottom left) led steeply down to the theater, which was terraced into the slopes beyond.

69–70. Verulanium (St. Albans, England) in the first and fourth centuries A.D. The stability of the street plan contrasts with the successive changes in the defensive circuits.

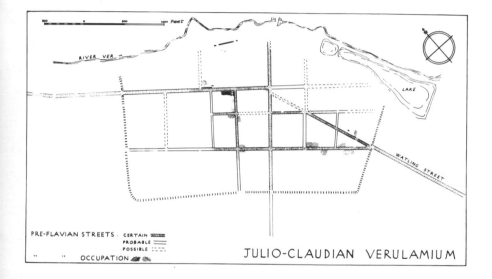

JULIO-CLAUDIAN VERULAMIUM

70.

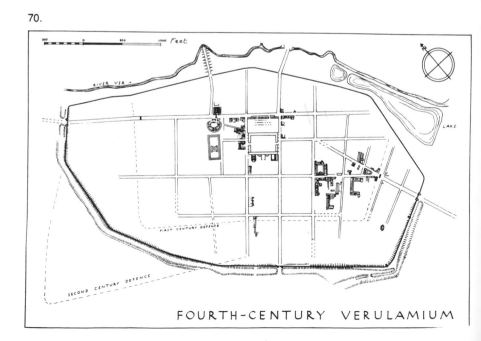

FOURTH-CENTURY VERULAMIUM

71–72. Calleva Atrebatorum (Silchester, England). The orthogonal street plan (second century A.D.) was superimposed on an earlier, less regular layout. The defenses visible in the air photograph are even later (about A.D. 200), excluding some of the existing street grid.

CALLEVA

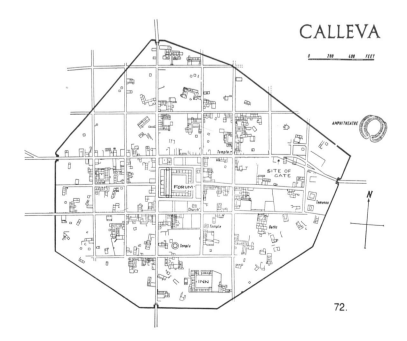

72.

73. Lepcis Magna (Tripolitania). Successive stages in the development of the street plan. 1, the pre-Roman nucleus; 2, the first Roman city; 3, after 8 B.C.; 4, early first century A.D.; 5, second century; 6, early third century.

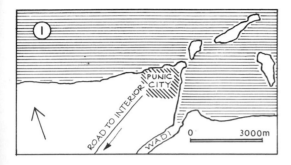

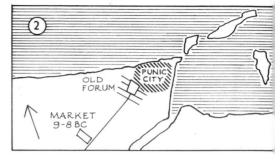

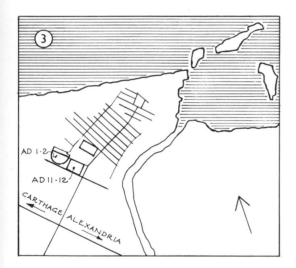

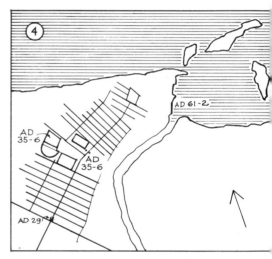

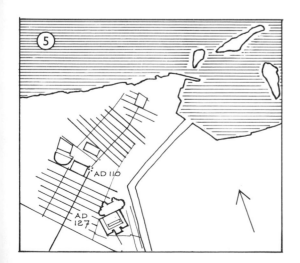

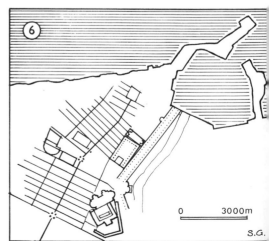

74. Lepcis Magna, the Old Forum. 1–3, temples (late first century B.C. to A.D. 14–19); 4, basilica (mid first century A.D.); 5, curia (seat of the municipal council, probably second century A.D.); 6, temple of Cybele (A.D. 71–2); 7, temple (about A.D. 100, later a church); 8, temple (A.D. 153); 9, line of sixth-century Byzantine defense. The forum was paved and surrounded by porticoes in A.D. 53–4.

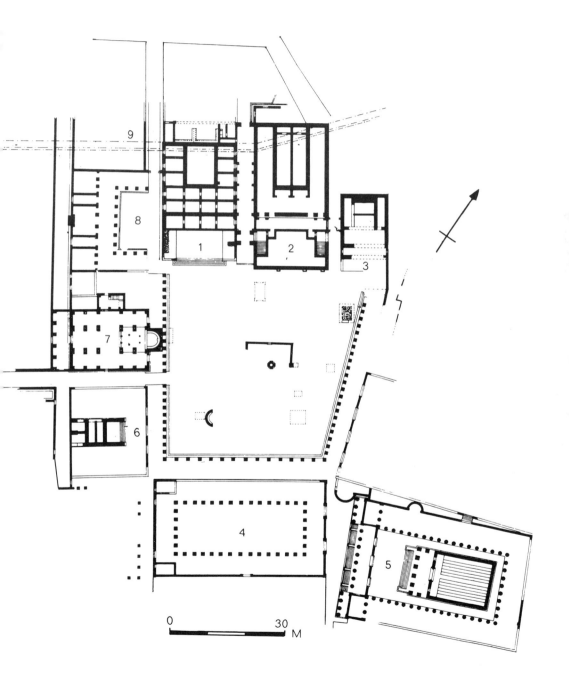

74a. Lepcis Magna. 1, Old Forum. 2–3, Hadrianic Baths (A.D. 123) and exercise ground (palaestra). 4, circular piazza and monumental fountain. 5, colonnaded street. 6, artificial harbor basin. 7–8, Severan Forum and Basilica. 4–8 were the creation of the Lepcis-born emperor Septimius Severus and his family (A.D. 193–217) (cf. Fig. 736).

Lighthouse

The Wadi Lebda

74b. Lepcis Magna.
1, Theater complex.
2, Market. 3, Old Forum.
4–5, Severan Forum and
Basilica. 6, The old road
to the interior along
which the successive
first-century
developments were laid
out (cf. Fig. 734).

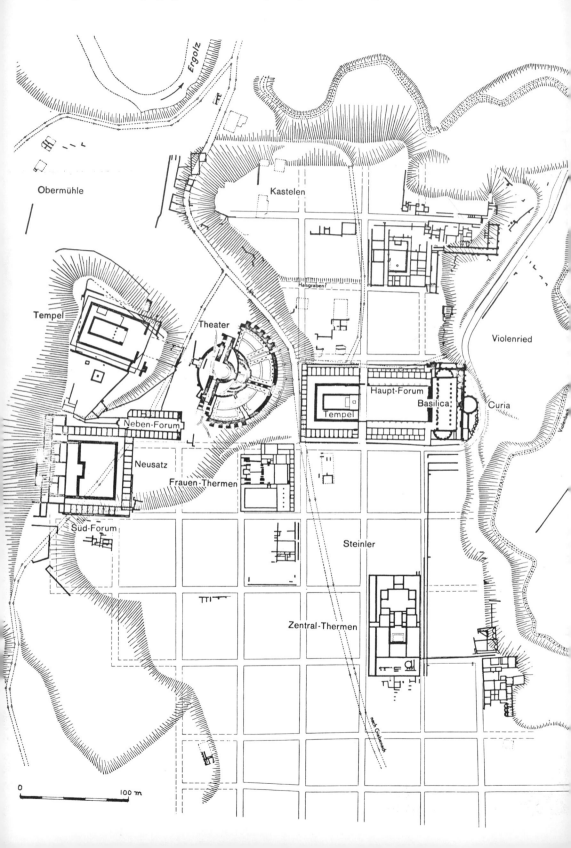

75. Augusta Raurica (Augst), near Basel. Military colony founded 43 B.C.

76. Augusta Raurica. The forum complex, rebuilt in its present form in the second century A.D. 1, temple and porticoed precinct (the stairs indicate a second story); 2, the open forum courtyard, flanked by porticoes and shops; 3, basilica; 4, curia, the seat of the town council, a third-century addition.

77. Augusta Raurica. The basilica-forum complex; the theater and beyond it, on axis, a temple; and (top left) a large covered market.

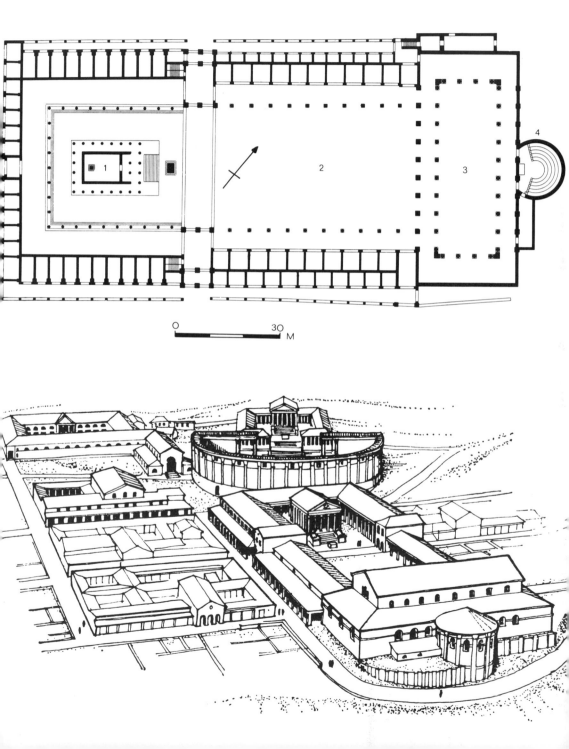

78. Iader (Zadar, Zara, Dalmatia). Military colony, about 33 B.C. The medieval and later town conserves the gridded Roman plan.

79. Pompeii. Basis of one of the secondary water tanks that supplied the individual city quarters. In the foreground a street-side bar.

80. Ostia. Public lavatory adjoining the Forum Baths, the waste water from which flushed the drains.

81. Sixth century B.C. rock-cut "cuniculus" near Veii. Similar channels were used widely both for water supply and for drainage.

82. Drain beneath one of the streets in the Roman Forum.

83. Ostia. Part of the riverside harbor quarter northwest of the Forum. 1, street flanked by shops and a portico with apartment house; 2–4, public warehouses; 5, three-story private warehouse; 6, shops fronting on to a covered street, with apartments over (cf. fig.51).

84. Part of the marble plan of Rome prepared about A.D. 200–210. It shows the juxtaposition of two commercial areas, one laid out on a regular grid, with street-side porticoes, many shops, a bath building (center left), and above it an apratment house, the other an area of irregular growth, including a large warehouse. The "V" symbols indicate staircases.

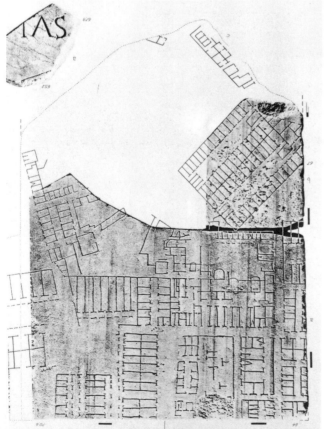

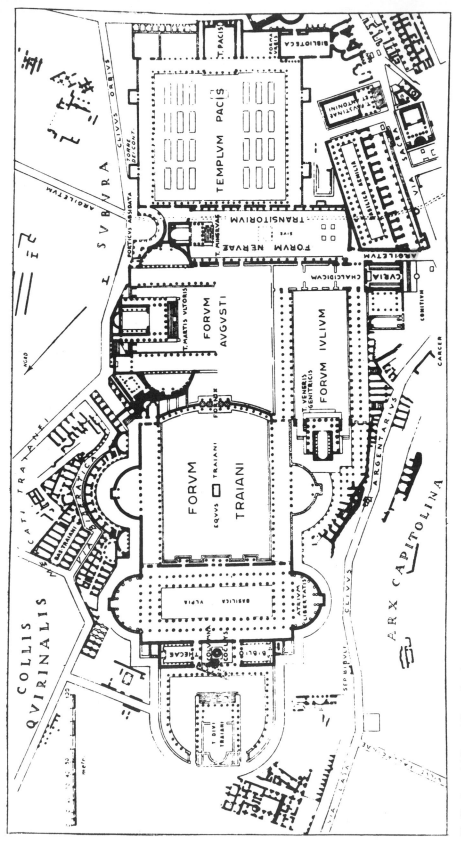

86. The Imperial Fora of Rome (as described in Appendix III).

NOTES

1. For the distinction between those Greek cities which grew and those which were founded on a single occasion, see Gerkan, pp.4–6. To the second category belong not only the majority of colonial foundations, but also the products of the phenomenon of formal *synoikismos*, whereby a number of towns or villages united to create a new and larger urban unit on a new site. Examples of this are Mantinea in Arcadia (464–59 B.C.), Rhodes (408–7 B.C.; see p. 19), and Megalopolis in Arcadia (371 B.C.). The earlier *synoikismoi* (as that of Attica, attributed to Theseus) involved the political, but not necessarily the physical, amalgamation of a number of small communities about a single, more powerful neighbor.

2. W. B. Dinsmoor, *The Architecture of Ancient Greece*, 3rd. ed. (1950) 8: "We have abundant literary and monumental evidence that the Greek temple, if not the lineal descendant of the Mycenaean palace, at least had an ancestry in common." The stoa-like "market" at Hagia Triada (Crete) is conveniently illustrated in *E.A.A.* III, Figs. 1385–6. Simple porticoes with wooden columns were certainly widely current in the later seventh and early sixth centuries B.C. (Larisa, Samos, Cyrene, Megara Hyblaea; see S. Stucchi, *L'Agora di Cirene* (Rome, 1965) 71–5; G. Vallet and F. Villard, *Mélanges d'Archéologie et d'Histoire*, (1969) 20. Only further excavation can tell whether such buildings represent any real measure of continuity or merely the re-emergence of simple building types well suited to the Greek climatic needs.

3. Kāhūn, the encampment for the builders of the pyramid of Sesostris II (ca. 1890 B.C.) at Illāhūn: W. M. F. Petrie, *Kāhūn, Gurob and Hawara*, London, 1890; *E.A.A.* IV, 287 and Fig. 340. Tell el-Amarna, the workmen's village (ca. 1370 B.C.): E. Peet and C. L. Woolley, *The City of Akhenaten* (London, 1923).

4. Second century A.D. Now being excavated by Dr. Friedrich Rakob.

5. Paul Lampl; *Cities and Planning in the Ancient Near East* (1968) 18, Fig. 33.

6. J. M. Cook and R. V. Nicholls in *Annual of the British School at Athens*, LIII–LIV (1958–59) 1–137. Old Smyrna lay to the north of the later town, round the bay, the modern Bayrakli.

7. For the known facts of the life of Hippodamos, see Castagnoli (1972) 66–72. The fullest source is Aristotle, *Politics*, II,1267b, cf. VII,1330b. The authority for his participation at Thurii is Hesychius. Unfortunately, I did not see McCredie (1971) until this book was in proof. He prefers a later chronology for Hippodamos, excluding Miletus but including Rhodes.

8. The independence of fortifications and street plan is emphasized by Horst de la Croix, *Military Considerations in City Planning: Fortifications*, p. 22.

9. The term *theatroeidēs* ("like a theater") used by Diodorus (XIX,45; XX,83) unquestionably refers to the configuration of the site, not, as has been suggested, to the disposition of the street plan; cf. Vitruvius (II,8,43) on the site of Halicarnassos. See also p. 19.

10. The terms *plateia* and *stenōpos* are well discussed by Castagnoli (1972) 32–4. The corresponding Latin terms are *platea* and *angiportus* (Vitruvius, I,6,1; cf. I,7,1). The use of *angiportus* for a blind alley (e.g., Varro, *de lingus latina* VI,41) is a secondary development; many such minor streets did have no exit. The terms *cardo (maximus)* and

decumanus (maximus), widely used by archaeologists to denote the N–S and E–W arteries of a Roman town, belong properly to the vocabulary of the Roman field surveyor (p. 27). As urban terms they are not attested in antiquity and are better avoided.

11. G. Klaffenbach, *Die Astynomen-Inschrift von Pergamon*, Berlin (1954); translated and commented by Martin (1956) 57–66.

12. *American Journal of Philology*, LV1 (1935) 359–72; *Revue Philologique* (1936) 158; Martin (1956) 55–6.

13. Of the canonical "Seven Wonders," only the statue of Zeus at Olympia was in metropolitan Greece, and even that was in the exotic medium of ivory and gold leaf.

14. Alinda: R. Martin, *Recherches sur l'Agora grecque* (Paris, 1951) 425, pls. VI–XI. Labranda: plan in *Acta Instituti Ath. Regni Sueciae*, V,1, pl. XXIV (cf. *E.A.A.* IV, 440–2). Pisidian Antioch: virtually unpublished (cf. *American Journal of Archaeology* XXVIII (1924) 434–444). Attaleia (Antalya), Kremna, Sagalassos, Termessos: K. Lanckoronski, *Städte Pamphyliens und Pisidiens* (Vienna, 1892).

15. See Castagnoli (1972) 132. The present street plan certainly antedates the city walls (late fifth century?) the main gates of which in turn indicate the established lines of the roads beyond. The principal anomalies are the slight but consistent clockwise displacement (about 2 degrees) of the orientation of the three sixth-century temples in relation to the streets, and the corresponding eastward displacement of the north gate, necessitating an awkward dogleg in the main N–S street. Both are explained if it may be assumed that the predecessor of this street was found to be slightly out of alignment and had to be corrected when the plan was formally "urbanized."

16. Poseidonia, see note 15. At Selinus there is a similar but less consistent obliquity of alignment in the temples on the acropolis.

17. E.g., in the fourth-century settlement (or resettlement) of Corcyra Nigra in the Adriatic; Dittenberger, *Sylloge* 3, 141. Aristotle (*Politics*, VII, 1330) envisages an allocation of two agricultural plots, one near the town and one more distant. For building plots within the town, see the decree regulating the fourth-century enlargement of Colophon (note 12).

18. Conveniently summarized by Aleksandra Wasowicz in *Mélanges de l'Ecole Française de Rome* (LXXXIV, 1972) 199–229, whence Fig. 37.

19. Few subjects have been the object of so much inconclusive erudition, much of which may now be left to the historian of religious belief and cosmic speculation. No amount of ingenuity can square the facts of Roman topography with Varro's statement (in Solinus, I,17) that Rome was originally "quartered" (*quadrata*) because it was laid out on a "balanced" plan (*quod ad aequilibrium foret posita*). Roma Quadrata, in the sense of an urban nucleus that was in some sense quartered, has been sought in vain on the Palatine and in the Forum—in vain, because it never existed. It was the product of late Republican antiquarian speculation, based in part on observation of such time-honoured religious practices as those which bequeathed the word "temple" (*templum*) to the language, and which were themselves compounded of a bewildering variety of superimposed layers of cosmic belief, ranging from Babylonia to Etruria and Hellenistic Greece; based in part also on the superficially similar practices of the Roman land surveyors, which in turn included an element of religious ritual (*posita auspicaliter groma*: Hyginus [ed. Lachmann] 170). The confusion was made easier by the many traditional religious practices involved in the formal establishment of a new Roman city, some of these probably Etruscan in origin (e.g., the taking of omens within a ritually quartered *templum*), others (e.g., the plowing of a furrow to mark the line of walls and gates and the reservation of an open zone [*pomerium*] between this line and the fields beyond) almost

certainly a heritage of the Latin peoples themselves. For a sensible and well-document-
ed summary of the problem, see Castagnoli (1972) 74–81; also S. Weinstock, *Journal of
Roman Studies*,XXXVI (1964) 101–129.

There is no longer any need to take seriously the belief, once widely held, that the
roots of Italian orthogonal planning are to be sought in the *terramare* settlements of the
northern Italian Bronze Age. See G. Patroni, *Athenaeum*, VIII (1930) 425–451, and G.
Säflund, *Le Terremare delle Provincie di Modena (Skrifter utgivna av Svenska Institut
i Rom*, VII (1939).

20. Veii: current excavations on the Piazza d'Armi, directed by G. Colonna; the formal layout
    dates from the sixth century. The plan of the city given by Gerkan (fig. 16) is pure fantasy.
    Acqua Rossa, near Viterbo: current Swedish excavations directed by C. E. Ostenberg.

    The assertion of Horst de la Croix (*op. cit.*, p. 26) that the cities of Etruria were
    distinguished from those of Greece by being artificially fortified from the outset is
    mistaken. They did tend to occupy sites with natural defenses, and many of them had an
    independently fortified acropolis; but as in Greece city walls enclosing the whole inhabit-
    ed area were quite a late development. In this respect Rome followed Etruscan practice.
    The earliest archaeological evidence for the occupation of the Capitoline Hill and its
    citadel, the Arx, dates from the sixth century B.C., and the "Servian" walls enclosing the
    town were even later. See Scullard (1967), pp. 78–79; also, for Veii, fortified only in the
    late fifth century, Ward-Perkins in *Papers of the British School at Rome*, XXXIX (1961)
    32.

21. Within this broadly Greek scheme the detailed planning reveals features that were not
    Greek: irregular planning of the individual blocks (contrast Olynthus, Fig. 11), distinctive
    types of houses.

22. See Castagnoli (1972) 96.

23. Dilke (1971) 68 (reproducing the illustration in Hyginus Gromaticus) and 155; cf. *Atlas
    des centuriations romaines de Tunisie* (Paris, 1954). A comparable example in Italy is
    the centuriation of Luca (Lucca).

24. Castagnoli (1972) Fig. 50, after P. Davin, *Revue Tunisienne*, 1 (1930) 73 ff.

25. On the site of the Flavian building. It awaits publication.

26. Grenier (1958) 236.

27. Grenier (1958) 246 (Nîmes); 227 and 232 (Lyon).

28. W. Ruesch in *Archaeologischer Anzeiger* (1962) 878.

29. For the city centers of these towns, see Ward-Perkins in *Journal of Roman Studies* LX
    (1970) 6–13.

30. Boethius and Ward-Perkins (1970) 399–402.

31. Boethius and Ward-Perkins (1970) 406 ff.

32. Boethius and Ward-Perkins (1970) 417 ff. The earliest example in the West, at Lepcis
    Magna (ca. A.D. 200), was planned by an architect from Asia Minor.

33. Boethius and Ward-Perkins (1970) 486–490.

34. E.g., at Priene, from a spring two miles away, Wiegand-Schrader (1904); at Olynthus,
    exceptionally, from eight miles,Robinson, XII (1946) 103–114.

35. Herodotus III, 60, 1. For the tunnel, 1045 meters long, see *Archaeologischer Anzeiger* (1960) 178–198.

36. A. Blanchet, *Recherches sur les aqueducs et cloaques de la Gaule romaine* (Paris, 1908) 7; cf. 80–86. The estimated figure for Imperial Rome is about 150 million gallons daily.

37. For the Athenian equivalent of "Gardyloo", see Aristophanes, *Acharnians*, 616–7: *existo*, "stand clear!" Strabo (XXXVI, 646) comments on the absence of covered sewers at Smyrna, a city he otherwise admired.

38. J. B. Ward-Perkins, "Etruscan engineering" in *Hommages à Albert Grenier* (Brussels, 1962) 1636–43.

39. Named, for example, in the Caesarian Lex Municipalis (Dessau, *Inscriptiones Latinae Selectae*, 6085; translated by E. G. Hardy, *Roman Laws and Charters* [Oxford, 1912] 136 ff.) the contents of which are assumed to concern all Italian municipalities.

40. The *forum pecuarium* (sheep market) of Ferentinum (*Corpus Inscriptionum Latinarum* I,2,5850) lay outside the walls, probably by the east gate (Fig. 43); Bartoli (1954) 479. Other markets outside or near the gates were the *macellum* at Lepcis Magna, when first built (Fig. 73c); the Market of Sertius at Thamugadi (partly visible in Fig. 66, bottom right); and the Oval Forum at Gerasa (Fig. 27).

41. For these market types, J. B. Ward-Perkins in *Journal of Roman Studies*, LX (1970) 15–16.

42. G. E. Rickman, *Roman Granaries and Store Buildings* (Cambridge, 1971).

43. *Annals* XV, 43.

44. G. Carettoni, et. al., *La Pianta Marmorea di Roma Antica* (Rome, 1960).

SELECT BIBLIOGRAPHY AND NOTES ON THE SITES ILLUSTRATED, TOGETHER WITH NOTES ON SOME OF THE PRINCIPAL SITES REFERRED TO IN TEXT

In the bibliography preference is given to works in the English language, where available. Under individual towns only monographs and a few important recent articles are cited. The single books referred to for Athens and for Rome were selected from a vast bibliography because they subsume all works previous to their dates of publication. Almost all the sites referred to will be found, with plans, in the appropriate volumes of *E.A.A.*; in the works of Castagnoli, Martin and Giuliano for the Greek-speaking world, including Sicily and southern Italy; and of Schmiedt for Italy. For sites referred to in text but not specifically listed below, see also notes to chapters and the notes at the head of each section of the following lists.

Dimensions in feet refer to the Roman foot (roughly equivalent to the modern foot). Other dimensions are given in meters.

BIBLIOGRAPHY

A.C.M. III. Acta Congressus Madvigiani (Proceedings II Int. Congr. of Classical Studies), vol. III, *Urbanism and Town Planning.* Copenhagen, 1958.

Blanckenhagen, P. von. "The Imperial Fora," in *Journal of the Society of Architectural Historians,* XIII (1954), pp. 21–26.

Boethius, A. and Ward-Perkins, J. B. *Etruscan and Roman Architecture.* London, 1970.

Boethius, A. "The Hellenized Italic Town" in *The Golden House of Nero.* Ann Arbor, 1960, pp. 26–93.

Bradford, J. S. P. *Ancient Landscapes.* London, 1957.

Castagnoli, F. *Orthogonal Town Planning in Antiquity.* Cambridge (Mass.) and London, 1972. A translation, with an Appendix (1970), of his *Ippodamo di Mileto e la Pianta Ortogonale;* cf. *Archeologia Classica,* XV (1963), pp. 180–97.

Dilke, O. A. W. *The Roman Land Surveyors.* Newton Abbot, 1971.

E.A.A. Enciclopedia dell'Arte Antica e Orientale, 7 vols. Rome, 1958–1966.

Gerkan, A. von. *Griechische Städteanlagen.* Berlin-Leipzig, 1924.

Giuliano, A. *Urbanistica delle Citta Greche.* Milan, 1966.

Grenier, A. *Manuel d'archéologie gallo-romaine,* vol. III,3. Paris, 1957.

Haverfield, F. *Ancient Town-planning.* Oxford, 1913.

Jones, A. H. M. *The Greek City from Alexander to Justinian.* Oxford, 1940.

Kraeling, C. "The Greek and Roman Orient" in *City Invincible: a symposium on urbanization and cultural development in the ancient Near East.* Chicago, 1960.

Martin, R. *L'Urbanisme dans la Grèce Antique.* Paris, 1956.

Mazzolani, L. S. *The Idea of the City in Roman Thought: from walled city to spiritual commonwealth.* Indiana University Press, Bloomington and London, 1970.

McCredie, J. R. "Hippodamos of Miletus," in *Studies Presented to George M. A. Hanfmann.* Mainz, 1971.

Nash, E. *A Pictorial Dictionary of Ancient Rome,* 2 vols., 2nd ed., New York, 1968 (with the best recent bibliography of the individual monuments).

Salmon, E. T. *Roman Colonization under the Republic.* London, 1969.

Schmiedt, G. *Atlante Aerofotografico delle Sedi Umane in Italia.* Florence, 1970.

Scullard, H. H. *The Etruscan Cities and Rome.* London, 1967.

Travlos, J. *Pictorial Dictionary of Ancient Athens.* Perlzweig, J., tr., New York, 1971.

Wycherley, R. E. *How the Greeks Built Cities.* London, 1949.

Ward-Perkins, J. B. "Early Roman Towns in Italy" in *Town Planning Review,* XXXVI (1955) pp. 127–54.

Of the above, Castagnoli and Martin are fundamental to their subject. Gerkan and Haverfield, though largely superseded in detail, were important pioneer works Schmiedt is an invaluable repertory of air photographs and plans. Though not concerned with city planning as such, Jones presents the political, cultural, and social background against which it developed in the Hellenistic and Roman East; and Mazzolani discusses what educated Romans thought about their towns—which, then as today, was by no means what was actually happening in them. For the similar gulf in Greece between theory and practice, see p. 37.

GREECE AND THE GREEK EAST
Most of the towns listed below are conveniently illustrated and discussed in Martin (1956), in Giuliano (1966), which derives closely from Martin, and in *E.A.A.*

AIGAI (northwest Asia Minor)
Figs. 16, 17. Rebuilt and enlarged in the early second century B.C. The site, which was developed under the strong influence of Attalid Pergamon, drops steeply towards the west in a series of monumental terraces. The upper two, the acropolis, and below it two temples and (on the east side) a market, occupy the site of the original town; below this the theater, with an adjoining terraced enclosure, porticoed at several levels; below this again the stadium. R. Bohn, *Altertümer von Aegae* (Berlin, 1908).

ANTIOCH-ON-THE-ORONTES (Antakya, southeastern Turkey, near the Syrian border)
Founded in 300 B.C. by Seleucus Nicator. Traces of the original street plan have been preserved by its Roman and later successors. Five avenues (the central one later colonnaded by Herod the Great) ran NE–SW between the Orontes and Mount Silpius, which served as an acropolis. At least 20 cross streets have been recognized. J. Lauffray in *A.C.M.* III, 8–10; G. Downey, *A History of Antioch in Syria* (Princeton, 1961).

APAMEA (north Syria, on the Orontes about 70 miles southwest of Aleppo)
Founded ca. 300 B.C. by Seleucus Nicator. The walls enclose an irregular area of 490 acres, with a single axial N–S avenue 23 meters wide, colonnaded in Roman times. In course of excavation. For the plan, see J. Lauffray in *A.C.M.* III, 11–12.

ASSOS (northwest Asia Minor)
Figs. 18, 19. Partially rebuilt on a fine terraced site in the early second century B.C. under the strong influence of Attalid Pergamon. Whereas the north stoa of the agora is cut back into the hillside, the multi-storied south stoa is both a terracing wall and a link with the much lower ground below. At the east end the council house (*bouleutrion*); at the west end a temple. F. H. Bacon, J. T. Clarke, R. Koldewey, *Investigations at Assos,* vol. 1 (1901).

ATHENS
See pp. 12, 13–24 and Figs. 3–5 for the development of the agora. For this and other topographical features, J. Travlos, *Pictorial Dictionary of Ancient Athens.* Perlzweig, J., tr. (New York, 1971).

BEROIA (Aleppo, northern Syria)
Founded by Seleucus Nicator between 301 and 281 B.C., incorporating a small earlier settlement. The modern street plan preserves elements of a Hippodamian grid with an axial E–W avenue, 20–25 meters wide. J. Sauvaget, *Alep* (Paris, 1941); J. Lauffray, *A.C.M.* III, 13–14.

DAMASCUS (Syria)
Fig. 21. The remodeling of this very ancient city may date from the second century B.C. (when it was briefly the capital of Syria), with subsequent Roman additions. The reconstructed plan is based on a study of the modern street plan in relation to the scattered surviving remains. Elements that are certain are the great sanctuary of Zeus (the Ummāyad Mosque) and the main axial street, colonnaded in Roman times ("the Street called Straight"). At the west end the walls incorporate part of the preclassical city. J. Sauvaget, Syria, XXVI (1949) 314–58.

DURA-EUROPOS (Syria, on the Euphrates 200 miles southeast of Aleppo)
See p. 20 and Figs. 22–25. The agora was originally planned to occupy eight city blocks (Fig. 22). Fig. 24 shows what was in fact completed and Fig. 25 the N.E. part of this as it appeared ca. A.D. 250. The small porticoed market place (Fig. 25, bottom left) was a Roman addition. For the site, see The Excavations at Dura-Europos. Preliminary Reports: First Season, 1927–28 (New Haven, 1929) and subsequent reports. For the agora, Ninth Season, part 1 (1944).

GERASA (Jerash, Jordania, about 100 miles south of Damascus)
Figs. 26, 27. Successively a native, a Seleucid, and a Roman city, the present layout dates from the third quarter of the first century A.D. The plan was constructed around the N–S axial colonnaded street; two transverse colonnaded streets; and the South Theater, an oval piazza (the "Forum," Fig. 27) and the temple of Zeus, which together represent the earlier inhabited nucleus. Dominating the whole was the temple of Artemis, with its monumental E–W processional approach. C. H. Kraeling, Gerasa, City of the Decapolis (New Haven, 1938); Boethius and Ward-Perkins (1970) 436–9.

GOURNIA (eastern Crete)
See p. 10 and Fig. 1. The layout of this small Late-Minoan town was determined by the location, along the crest of a rocky ridge, of a palace and of the public forecourt adjoining it. The only other public building is a small shrine, north of the palace. H. Boyd-Hawes, Gournia Vasiliki and other Prehistoric Sites (American Exploration Society, 1908); R. W. Hutchinson, Town Planning Review, XXI (1950) 215–7, Fig. 21

HALICARNASSOS (Bodrum, southwest Asia Minor)
See p. 19. Martin (1956) 147–51.

KARPHI (eastern Crete)
Fig. 2. Small town (estimated population 3,000–4,000) established by refugees from the collapse of the Cretan Bronze Age civilization on a precipitous rocky saddle, 1,300 feet above the plain of Lasithi. The individual houses represent a decadent Minoan tradition, but there is no central palace, as at Gournia, to give a semblance of order to the plan. The only recognizable public building is a temple at the northern extremity of the main group. Annual of the British School at Athens, XXXVIII (1940) 57–145; R. W. Hutchinson, Town Planning Review, XXI (1950) Fig. 22.

KNIDOS (the extreme southwest promontory of Asia Minor)
Refounded, probably in the fourth century B.C., on terraced, sharply rising ground, facing a rocky island, which was artificially linked to the mainland to form two harbors. As at Priene the site is dominated by the rocky cliffs that carried the city wall up to the acropolis, with the finely sited Greek theater looking out across the town. The layout was based on a grid of E–W streets, with one dominant avenue, intersected by a number of steep N–S streets, most of which were stepped up the lower slopes. For the recent excavations, see reports in American Journal of Archaeology since vol. LXXIII (1969). The best available plans (Gerkan, Fig. 10; E.A.A. II, Fig. 966) derive from that of C. T. Newton, Halicarnassos, Cnidus and Branchidae, pl. 50.

LAODICEIA-ON-THE-SEA (Latakieh, Syria, on the coast 90 miles southwest of Aleppo)
Fig. 20. Port city for Apamea, founded by Antiochus II (287–247 B.C.). The modern street plan

and remains of street-side colonnades (presumably of Roman date) indicate an orthogonal plan with one N–S axial avenue and at least three transverse avenues. The irregular wall circuit encloses an area of about 530 acres. J. Sauvaget, *Bulletin des Etudes Orientales*, IV (1935) 81–114; J. Lauffray, *A.C.M.* III, 12–13.

MANTINEA (Arcadia)
Founded ca. 465 B.C. by the *synoikismos* (act of union) of five villages; destroyed by the Spartans soon after 385, but rebuilt on approximately the same lines in 370 (Pausanias, VIII,8,9; Xenophon, *Hell.* VI,5,5). Despite the unusual elliptical circuit of the defenses, the street plan approximates to orthogonal. This was not a radiating plan. G. Fougères, *Mantinée et l'Arcadie Orientale* (Paris, 1898) 115 ff.

MEGALOPOLIS (Arcadia)
Founded in 371 B.C. as federal capital of the Arcadian League (Diodorus XV,94; Pausanias VIII,27,7). The layout reflected its double role: on the south bank of the river Helisson the federal buildings (theater, assembly hall, federal cults) and on the north bank those of the municipality (agora, gymnasium, local cults). R. Gardner, *Excavations at Megalopolis* (London, 1892).

MILETUS (Asia Minor, at the mouth of the river Maeander)
See p. 14 and Figs. 7–10. Refounded in or soon after 479 B.C. The slight difference in orientation (about 1 degree) between the street layouts to the north and south of the reserved belt of public land may be due to the fact the former appears to repeat a previous orthogonal layout, prior to the city's destruction in 494 B.C. The northern half incorporates a single transverse avenue, 7.5 meters wide, the southern half two intersecting avenues of the same size. Note how the longitudinal avenue had to dogleg in order to emerge from the independently sited city walls. Outside the public monuments much of the plan is based on isolated soundings. Martin (p. 123) and others (e.g., G. Colonna in *E.A.A.* IV,14) suggest that many of the housing blocks, particularly in the south quarter, were of the more familiar elongated rectangular pattern, but it is hard to square this suggestion with the plan as published. A detailed restatement of the archaeological evidence would be welcome. Milet: *Ergebnisse d. Ausgrabungen seit d. Jahre 1899*, vol. 1 (Berlin, 1906) and subsequent volumes; Gerkan, *passim*, esp. p. 38 ff. G. Kleiner, *Die Ruinen von Milet* (Berlin, 1968) is a convenient handbook with classified bibliography.

For the defenses, see Horst de la Croix, *Military Considerations in City Planning: Fortifications*, pp. 25–26. The fifth-century circuit linked the inhabited area to an independently fortified acropolis, as in many classical Greek towns (e.g., Corinth, Knidos, Priene), whereas the later circuit (ca. 200 B.C.) left the acropolis outside, relying instead upon a more dynamic concept of mobile defense and upon subtleties of siting. In both cases the lack of any close organic link between the defenses and the layout of the inhabited area made it easier to plan the former in accordance with the best contemporary military thinking.

OLYNTHUS (northern Greece, 30 miles southeast of Thessaloniki)
See p. 15 and Figs. 11, 11a. Refounded ca. 432 B.C.; destroyed in 348 B.C. The new town was based on a scheme of two N–S avenues, one 5 meters and one 7 meters wide, divided by a number of cross streets into uniform housing blocks, each measuring 120 by 300 feet, and subdivided longitudinally by a narrow alleyway. D. M. Robinson, *Excavations at Olynthus*, vols. II, VIII, and XIII (Baltimore, 1930, 1938, and 1946).

PEIRAEUS (the harbor town of Athens)
See p. 16. Laid out by Hippodamos (Aristotle, *Politics* II, 1267b22; cf. Xenophon, *Hellenica* II,4,11) shortly after the Persian wars (so Scholiast to Aristophanes, *Knights*, 327). For the known remains, which were evidently orthogonally disposed and included one avenue 14 to 15 meters wide, see W. Judeich, *Topographie von Athen* (Munich, 1931), plan III; other fuller "restorations" of the plan are speculative. For the boundary stones, see: *Inscriptiones Graecae*, I,[2] 887–896; D. K. Hill, *American Journal of Archaeology*, XXXVI (1932) 254–259; Martin (1956) 106–10, with schematic plan of the zoning.

PERGAMON (Bergama, northwest Asia Minor)
See p. 18 and Figs. 14, 15. *Altertümer von Pergamon*, vol. 1 (Berlin, 1912), and subsequent volumes.

PERGE (Pamphylia, on the south coast of Asia Minor)
Fig. 28. In or soon after A.D. 117–122 the wide axial avenue of the Hellenistic city was given lateral porticoes and a central water channel to create a grandiose colonnaded street, focused upon the old South Gate of the city, the inner courtyard of which was embellished with statuary and a monumental triple arch. K. Lanckoronski, *Städte Pamphyliens und Pisidiens*, vol. 1 (Vienna, 1890) 33–63; A. M. Mansel, *Archaeologischer Anzeiger* (1956) 99–120.

PRIENE (southwest Asia Minor)
See p. 15 and Figs. 12, 12a, 12b. Refounded ca. 350 B.C. on a new site overlooking the river Maeander. The basis of the layout is a network of housing blocks, each 120 by 160 feet, with two principal longitudinal avenues, 5.60 to 7.35 meters wide; many of the lesser streets are stepped. The gymnasium and stadium are incorporated within the walls, the latter aligned obliquely so as to secure a level surface. T. Wiegand and H. Schrader, *Priene* (Berlin, 1904); M. Schede, *Die Ruinen von Priene* (Berlin, 1934).

RHODES
See p. 15 and Fig. 13. Founded in 408–7 B.C. on a new site, as an act of union between the three cities of Ialysos, Kamiros, and Lindos. The plan was universally admired in antiquity, but its attribution by Strabo (XIV,654) to "the same architect as the Peiraeus," i.e., to Hippodamos, is chronologically impossible. Older theories of a radiating plan are based on a misinterpretation of Diodorus (XIX, 45; cf. XX, 83); see p. 19. For the orthogonal plan, see I. D. Kondis, *Athenische Mitteilungen*, LXXIII (1958) 146 ff.; J. S. P. Bradford, *Antiquaries Journal*, XXXVI (1956) 57 ff.

THE GREEK WEST (SICILY AND MAGNA GRAECIA) AND ETRURIA

For individual sites not mentioned below, and for further details of most of these mentioned, see Castagnoli (1972), *E.A.A.* vols. 1–7, and Schmiedt.

AKRAGAS (Agrigento, S. Sicily)
Figs. 32–33. Greek colony, founded in 580 B.C. on a site of which the acropolis, to the north, and the ring of low cliffs followed by the city walls formed a natural amphitheater, within which the main inhabited area could be laid out on an orderly orthogonal scheme of E–W avenues (at least one is over 10 meters wide) with narrower cross streets (averaging 5 meters) and long, narrow domestic blocks. The layout must date from the city's foundation. The excavated quarter (Fig. 33) is of late second-century date, but beneath it lie similarly oriented structures of the sixth century; see E. De Moro in *Rendiconti dell'Accademia dei Lincei* XII (1957), 138 ff.

CAPUA (S. Maria Capua Vetere, Campania)
Successively the center of Etruscan power in the south, occupied ca. 425 B.C. by the Campani, and after 338 B.C. subjected to Rome. The one absolutely certain fact about its orthogonal plan is that it antedates the building of the Via Appia in 220 B.C. By far the most likely date for it is the heyday of Etruscan expansion in the sixth century B.C. The reconstructed plan proposed by Castagnoli from air photographs (Castagnoli (1972) 46–51, Fig. 20) is directly based on Greek models, with five or six broad E–W avenues and a large number of smaller transverse streets, the whole defended by an irregular circuit of walls enclosing some 400 acres. The streets are exactly oriented.

HERACLEA (Policoro, S. Italy)
Fig. 36. Greek colony on the Gulf of Taranto, S.W. of Metapontum, founded in 433–2 B.C. The

plan (based on air photographs and confirmed by excavation) comprises two elements: a long, narrow, natural promontory on which were the acropolis and the agora, and, across the slopes of the shallow valley to the south, an orthogonal layout of streets enclosed within a neatly rectangular city wall. L. Quilici, *Siris-Heraclea* (*Forma Italiae, Regio III*, vol. 1) Rome (1967) 159–186. Recent excavation has exposed the agora near the N.W. corner.

MARZABOTTO (N. Italy, 12 miles S.W. of Bologna)

Fig. 42. Founded by the Etruscans, about 500 B.C., to control the important trans-Apennine route down the river Reno; destroyed by the Gauls in the early fourth century. The site comprises an acropolis and a lower town. The latter was laid out on the level river terrace (now considerably eroded) and it incorporated three major E–W avenues (15 meters wide), crossed at right angles by one N–S avenue. In this it follows Greek models; but although the lesser streets were parallel, running E–W, neither the residential blocks nor the subdivisions thereof followed a regular plan. There was elaborate provision for both domestic and street drainage. A notable feature is the precision of the orientation, and at two of the street intersections the excavators have found the flat stones marking the stations for the surveyor's *groma*. The more recent excavations await detailed publication; summaries in *E.A.A.* IV (1961) 896–9 and in *Melanges de l'Ecole Française de Rome, LXXXIV (1972) 111–144.*

MEGARA HYBLAEA (Sicily)

Figs. 34–35. Founded ca. 750 B.C. and destroyed by the Syracusans in 483; though reoccupied later, it was never again of any importance. The formal layout dates from the second half of the seventh century; see above, p. 23. For a convenient summary of the results of the postwar excavations, see G. Vallet, F. Villard and P. Auberson, *Annales* (1970) 1102–1113.

METAPONTUM (southern Italy)

Fig. 38. Greek colony, established ca. 600 B.C. on the Gulf of Taranto. Air photography and sample excavation have revealed the plan of the city, with broad E–W avenues intersected by at least two N–S avenues and a number of narrower streets, and enclosed within an irregular wall circuit beside the (now-silted-up) harbor. For the accompanying field systems (above, p. 24) see most recently R. Uggeri in *Parola del Passato* XXIV (1969) 51–7, recording survey and extensive sample excavation of the system on the Bradano-Basento plateau. The visible surface indications, showing a longitudinal division into a series of uniform strips 205 meters wide, are due to a series of field-boundary drainage ditches. They were not cut until about 470–460 B.C., but they perpetuate the longitudinal elements of an earlier system of orthogonal tracks, field boundaries and farms which, wherever sampled, go back to the mid sixth century. The larger transverse divisions seem to have been 323 meters apart, giving major units of 60 Greek *schoinoi* (30 Roman *jugera*), which may or may not represent the original property holdings. For comparison, note that the standard Roman "century" (p. 28) comprised 200 *jugera* (about 25 acres), the basic small holding being 2 *jugera* (1 *haeredium*, or heritable plot) and the century being 100 such *haeredia*. The earliest Roman colonists (e.g., at Tarracina in 329 B.C.) received just this (2 *jugera*). Later allotments were often much larger.

NEAPOLIS (Naples)

Fig. 39. The original Greek settlement occupied the promontory of Pizzofalcone, west of the modern port. The "New Town" (*Neapolis*), a creation of the mid fifth century, lay to the north of the port, on the same site as the medieval city, the street plan of which was substantially that of the classical town. Air photographs clearly show three of the four E–W avenues (*plateiai*) and the numerous N–S cross streets, several of which were probably also *plateiai*; cf. the near-contemporary Thurii. Many of the streets were still known in the Middle Ages by the classical names *platea* and *vicus*. The widening of the N–S Via del Duomo, (near the center) is a modern feature.

POMPEII (Campania, Bay of Naples)

Figs. 40, 41, 79. A small native town, founded in the sixth century B.C. at the mouth of the river Sarno, in close contact with both Greeks and Etruscans. Conquered by the Samnites (ca. 425) and Romans, it became a Roman colony ca. 80 B.C. It was totally destroyed by the eruption of A.D. 79. Although the detailed evolution of the plan is still disputed, it is universally accepted that the original nucleus lay at the S.W. angle with a near-orthogonal plan based on two intersecting axial streets; the curving circuit of walls overlooked the shallow valley up which ran the coast road from Stabia to Naples, skirting the early settlement. The subsequent development is best regarded as a single event, contemporary with the establishment of a new and much larger wall circuit, probably under Greek influence soon after the battle of Cuma in 474 B.C. The anomalies of the plan stem from the incorporation of a number of pre-existing suburban roads. See most recently Hans Eschebach, *Die Städtebauliche des antiken Pompeji* (Heidelberg, 1970). His subdivision of the early town into two successive phases is, however, very questionable.

POSEIDONIA (Paestum, Gulf of Salerno)
Figs. 29, 30. Greek colony, founded ca. 700 B.C.; conquered by the Lucanians in the late fifth century, and refounded in 273 B.C. as the Roman military colony of Paestum. The date both of the walls and of the orthogonal street plan (which must antedate the walls) is disputed. The most likely date for the former seems to be late Greek or Lucanian, whereas the street plan as we now have it is probably of the later sixth century (see Castagnoli [1963] 187-190). The street plan, first observed in air photographs, is confirmed by excavation. As at Selinus there was a central zone reserved for public buildings. Within this zone the temples are consistently about 2 degrees out of alignment, while the north gate is correspondingly displaced to the east of its logical position. These facts suggest that, as at Megara Hyblaea (p. 23), there may have been an earlier layout, of the same general character but less mathematically precise, which needed slight correction when the city was formally "urbanized" in the later sixth century. (See also note 15.)

SELINUS (p. 23), Sicily)
Fig. 31. The westernmost Greek colony on the south coast, founded in 628 B.C. and destroyed by the Carthaginians in 409. Although the upper town was reoccupied in the fourth century it was never again a city of importance. The plan is discussed above (p. 24). As at Paestum, a strip of land was reserved for public use, on which are sited two of the early temples, both very slightly off-axis to, and probably therefore antedating, the formal "urbanization" of the initial colonial scheme. The date of this event was finally established by the excavations of I. Bovio Marconi (*Atti del VII Congresso Internazionale di Archeologia Classica*, vol. 2 [Rome, 1961], 11 ff.), showing that the fourth-century residential blocks rest on the footings of an identical sixth-century layout; see also E. Gabrici in *Monumenti Antichi*, XXXIII (1930) 61 ff.

THURII
Founded in 444-3 B.C. on or near the site of Sybaris. The plan is known only from the description in Diodorus XII,10,7. Its pan-Hellenic character and the participation of Hippodamos give it a special importance in relation to contemporary planning theory. It is discussed by Martin (1956) 40-1; Castagnoli (1972) 18-19, 131.

ITALY AND THE ROMAN WEST

For individual sites referred to in text but not listed below: for Italy, see Castagnoli (1972), *E.A.A.* vols. 1-7 (listed under their modern names) and Schmiedt; for the provinces, see notes to chapters.

ARAUSIO (Orange, Provence)
Figs. 47, 48. Reconstructed panel from the second of three successive cadastral plans, inscribed on marble for public display as a record of the legal and fiscal status of the centuriated subdivisions of the city's territory (cf. p. 35). The survey goes back to the foundation of the colony (ca. 35 B.C.), but this panel dates from about A.D. 100. It should be read as if facing west, with north to the right; and it illustrates an area on the east bank of the Rhone (just visible at the top) north of Pierrelatte; up the center flows the river Berre, in its old

course before canalization, and obliquely across the lower part the line of the main road to the north, shown as broken off where it enters hilly country. The squares indicate "centuries" (*centuriae*) of 2400 by 2400 Roman feet (20 by 20 *actus*), and the letters at the top of each square indicate its position in relation to the two basic grid lines of the survey, the N–S *kardo maximus* (which crosses this slab horizontally near the bottom) and the E–W *decumanus maximus* (which lay well to the left, i.e., south). Thus, D.D. XVIII C.K.II (bottom center) is an abbreviated version of *D(extra) D(ecumanum)* XVIII, *C(itra) K(ardinem)* II, indicating the eighteenth "century" to the right (north) of the E–W axis and the second "on this side" (east) of the N–S axis. The equivalent terms to the south and west respectively are *S(inistra) D.* and *V(ltra) K.* The remaining entries record the juridical and fiscal status and the rents due. A. Piganiol, *Les documents cadastraux de la colonie romaine d'Orange* (*Gallia*, Suppl. 16; Paris, 1962); cf. Dilke (1971) 159–77.

AUGUSTA PRAETORIA (Aosta, northern Italy)
Figs. 52–53. A veteran colony, just under 100 acres in extent, established in 25 B.C. near the head of the narrow valley that controls two of the Alpine passes into newly conquered Gaul. Although military engineers and surveyors were frequently called in to help, especially in the frontier provinces, this is one of the few examples of probable military influence on the actual plan, most clearly visible in the displacement of the transverse axis, just as in the standard contemporary military camp layout. The plan is based on one prepared in 1933 and published by P. Barocelli in *Aosta* (Ivrea, 1936). The Roman basis of the street plan is confirmed by numerous finds of the corresponding network of street drains.

AUGUSTA RAURICA (Augst, near Basel)
Figs. 75–77. Founded as a military colony in 43 B.C. A good example of a town of which the outer, originally fortified perimeter was as irregular (following the edge of the plateau) as the basic street grid was regular. The basilica-forum-temple complex, though itself of second-century date, exemplifies a planning formula which, first developed in Republican Italy, was diffused thence throughout the western provinces (note 29). Note that the forum was closed to vehicular traffic. Other standard Roman building types represented are the theater and two public baths. See R . Laur-Belart, *Führer durch Augusta Raurica* (Basel, 1948).

CALLEVA ATREBATORUM (Silchester, Britain)
Figs. 71, 72. A pre-Roman tribal capital, the Roman plan of which represents 150 years of gradual development within the framework of three successive circuits of defenses: an early rampart (just before or after A.D. 43), of which the most conspicuous trace in the later plan is the southward swing of the axial west-east street at the site of the earlier east gate; an outer earthwork (later first century A.D.), enclosing an area of 230 acres, which in the event proved overambitious; and a city wall (ca. A.D. 200) enclosing the effectively inhabited area of 105 acres. The orthogonal street plan, which antedates and extends beyond the latest defenses, was itself superimposed upon an earlier, less rigidly planned layout, which left its mark in the Forum (ca. A.D. 70) and the road running east from it, both slightly out of alignment to the later plan, and in the irregular siting of many of the peripheral buildings. This was a small country town, and only the main street frontages were ever fully built up. See George C. Boon, *Roman Silchester* (London, 1957).

COMUM, NOVUM COMUM (Como, northern Italy)
Figs. 56, 57. Refounded, or founded on a new site, during the first century B.C. An unusually clear example of an orthogonal street plan and rectangular wall circuit preserved with very little change by the medieval town. The irregular housing blocks which break the line of the axial street near the center probably mark the site of the forum.

COSA (Ansedonia, on the coast 80 miles N.W. of Rome)
Fig. 45. A Roman military colony, founded in 273 B.C. to control this sector of the Etruscan coast. The site is a commanding rocky hill, and the plan is an ingenious compromise between the demands of the freely sited defensive circuit and of an orthogonal street layout cleverly adapted to the contours of the sloping ground within the walls. The main coast road, the Via

Aurelia, bypassed the site on lower ground, and the later history of the town was largely one of a steady population drift down towards the road and the settlement beside the port. See F. E. Brown, *Cosa* 1 (*Memoirs of the American Academy in Rome*, XX, 1951).

CUICUL (Djemila, Algeria, about 70 miles north-west of Thamugadi)
Figs. 67, 68. A colony of military veterans founded in A.D. 96–7 on the road from Cirta (Constantine) to Sitifis (Sétif). The site chosen, the sloping crest of a sharply-defined triangular spur, accessible from the higher ground to the south only at one point (that occupied by the south gate), precluded a strictly orthogonal plan. As at Thamugadi the forum occupied a square central platform. An open stretch of ground outside the south gate served as a fairground and market, and beyond it there rapidly grew up a flourishing suburb, including a large bath building (A.D. 183) and, terraced down the eastern slopes, a theater (A.D. 161). About A.D. 216 the open space was formalized as a new and larger forum by the addition of a monumental arch and (Fig. 68) a temple to the reigning Severan Family (A.D. 229). Louis Leschi, *Djemila* (Algiers, 1953); P.A. Février, *Djemila* (Algiers, 1971).

FERENTINUM (Ferentino, 40 miles S.S.E. of Rome)
Figs. 43, 44. An ancient city of the Hernici, finely situated on a rocky hilltop, dominating the valley of the river Sacco and the Via Latina. The initial siting of both the city walls (fourth century B.C. onwards) and the terraced streets and buildings was determined almost exclusively by the natural configuration of the ground. The dominating terraces of the acropolis (late second century B.C.) mark the introduction of more sophisticated ideas of planning; perhaps also the forum area, which awaits detailed exploration. See A. Bartoli in *Rendiconti dell'Accademia dei Lincei*, IX (1954) 470–506.

FORUM CORNELII (Imola, northern Italy)
Fig. 46 illustrates a notable example of the survival of the regular centuriation pattern established by the Roman land surveyors, in this instance at some date after the establishment of the Via Aemilia in 187 B.C., upon the line of which the centuriation is based.

FORUM LIVI (Forli, northern Italy)
Fig. 63. Administrative center and market town, established on the Via Aemilia shortly after its construction in 187 B.C. at the point where two long-established trans-Apennine routes (northwards from Arezzo across the Mandrioli Pass, and northwestwards from Florence across the Muraglione Pass) converged and continued together northeastwards, across the plain towards Ravenna. The controlling factors in the development of the plan were the line of the Via Aemilia and the courses of two streams (since canalized and diverted) which enclosed a relatively small area in the middle of the larger medieval city. Visible in the photograph are several *limites* of a centuriated field system based on the line of the Via Aemilia. G. A. Mansuelli, *Caesena, Forum Popili, Forum Livi* (*Italia Romana: Municipi e Colonie*, series 2, III, Rome, 1948).

IADER (Zadar, Zara, Dalmatia)
Fig. 78. Refounded as a military colony by Augustus (about 33 B.C.) on a rocky promontory with a fine natural harbor. The neatly orthogonal plan is substantially that of the Augustan foundation. The centuriation of the adjoining mainland, though slightly differently oriented, is contemporary. J. J. Wilkes in *Dalmatia* (London, 1969) 206 ff.

LEPCIS (LEPTIS) MAGNA (Tripolitania)
Figs. 73, 74, 74a, 74b. Founded by the Carthaginians as a trading post in the sixth century B.C. beside one of the few natural harbors of this coast, it became one of the largest and wealthiest cities of Roman Africa. Its initial development under Roman rule (Fig. 73 1–4) was shaped by the existence of this primitive nucleus and by the gently curving course of the road that ran inland from it, up the low ridge west of the Wadi Lebda towards the farmlands and caravan routes of the interior, the sources of the city's wealth. The piecemeal development along this line is a classic example of successive failures to anticipate the rapidity of the city's growth. By the mid first century it had met and crossed at right angles the line of the arterial coast road from Carthage to Alexandria. The second century saw the consolidation of this

plan by the occupation of vacant areas to west and east (Fig. 73 5, the Hadrianic Baths, A.D. 123). The final stage (Fig. 73 6), took place under the Lepcis-born emperor, Septimius Severus (A.D. 193–211), who sponsored a grandiose redevelopment scheme, which included the creation of a large artificial harbor basin and a new civic center. This new quarter was an outstanding example of the skillful use of a potentially awkward site, the forerunner of the vast redevelopment projects of late antiquity of which Constantinople is the outstanding example. For the Old Forum (Figs. 74, 74a, 74b), see p. 30.

LUCA (Lucca, Tuscany)
Figs. 60–62. The layout of the medieval town has faithfully preserved the gridded streets and rectangular wall circuit of its Roman predecessor (date uncertain) and is in its turn preserved within the irregular oval circuit of the sixteenth-century defenses. The central piazza, around the church of S. Michele, marks the site of the forum, the oval piazza just north of the northeast corner of the Roman town the site of the amphitheater, now a marketplace. The central street intersection served also as the base point for the centuriation of the surrounding territory (Dilke [1971] 88).

OSTIA
Figs. 49–51, 80, 83, 85. Founded in the late fourth century B.C. as a military colony to defend the mouth of the Tiber, it prospered and grew as the seagoing port of Rome. The original walled settlement was small (5 acres) and neatly rectangular in plan, divided into four equal quadrants by two intersecting streets. About this nucleus the subsequent growth was dominated by the lines of the roads radiating from the early gates. To the north and east these roads prolonged the lines of the streets of the colony, facilitating a tidy orthogonal development (Fig. 83). To the south and west later builders had to be content with rationalizing the results of an initially unplanned ribbon development (Fig. 50); cf. Thamugadi, Fig. 65.

Fig. 50 illustrates the quarter outside the west gate: immediately outside, on the right, a public fountain and, on the left, a fish and meat market and a fuller's establishment (*fullonica*); between the two outer streets, a temple and a fourth-century church (*bottom left*), a market building, a temple of Mithras, and a bath building; and along the street frontages, shops and stairs to upper-story apartments . Along the street to the south of the gate the shops open off a street-side portico. See G. Becatti in *Scavi di Ostia*, vol. 1 (Rome, 1953).

PLACENTIA (Piacenza, northern Italy)
Fig. 54. Military colony established on the river Po, in 218 B.C., to control an important river crossing and port. In 190 it was reinforced, and in 187 it was linked with Ariminum (Rimini) by the great frontier highway, the Via Aemilia. It was presumably on this occasion that the town was laid out on a grid of which the two intersecting axes were the Via Aemilia and the road crossing the Po. Outside the west gate a third road continued up-river, on a slightly different alignment. The Roman and medieval nucleus and its access roads are still clearly visible within the larger area enclosed by the sixteenth-century defenses.

ROME
Figs. 82, 84, 86. Nash, E. *A Pictorial Dictionary of Ancient Rome*, 2 vols. (New York, 1968).

THAMUGADI (Timgad, Algeria, about 70 miles south of Constantine)
Figs. 65, 66. A colony of military veterans founded in 100 B.C. to control a strategic frontier defile. The rigidly orthogonal plan of the original settlement (about 25 acres) betrays the hand of a military surveyor from the nearby Third Legion, at Lambaesis, but in other respects this was a typical small Roman provincial town. Within less than a century it had more than doubled in size, spreading piecemeal along the roads outside the gates. Fig. 66 shows one such road in the foreground leading to a monumental arch (late second century) on the site of the original west gate; beyond it, the forum (left) and the theater. Jean Lassus, *Timgad* (Algiers, 1953); republished as *Visite a Timgad* (Algiers, 1969).

TICINUM (Pavia, northern Italy)
Fig. 55. An ancient Ligurian and Gaulish town which became a Roman *municipium* in 49 B.C. Controlling a crossing of the river Ticino, it was an important road junction on the road from

Placentia and the Via Aemilia to Augusta Praetoria and the Alpine passes, with easy access also to Mediolanum (Milan). Although it grew steadily in importance in late antiquity and the early Middle Ages, becoming for a time the capital of the Lombard Duchy of North Italy, it retained, little changed, its Roman street grid (49 B.C.? Augustan?), which shaped, and was in return conserved by, the successive late antique and medieval wall circuits. The present bridge occupies the site of its Roman predecessor. See D. A. Bullough in *Papers of the British School at Rome*, XXXIV (1966) 82–129.

VERONA (northern Italy)
Figs. 58–59. An important road center and crossing of the river Adige. The early town probably occupied the hill north of the bridge. Refounded (by Augustus?) on level ground in the loop of the river, with a regular grid of streets which has changed little since classical times. Two gates mark the line of the walls, which were restored, and slightly enlarged to incorporate the amphitheater, in A.D. 265. The central Piazza delle Erbe marks the site of the forum. F. Zorzi and others, *Verona e il suo territorio*, vol. 1 (Verona, 1961).

VERULAMIUM (St. Albans, Britain)
Figs. 69, 70. The capital of Belgic Britain, refounded after the Roman conquest of A.D. 43 on a fresh site, on level ground beside the ford which carried Watling Street, the main line of advance of the Roman armies, across the river Ver. The original street layout incorporated a stretch of this road, but was otherwise developed on orthogonal lines. In contrast to the stability of the street plan, there were (as at Calleva, Figs. 71–72) considerable fluctuations in the successive defensive circuits. Conveniently summarized by S. S. Frere in *Britannia Romana* (Rome, Accademia dei Lincei, 1971).

INDEX

SOURCES OF ILLUSTRATIONS

The author wishes to express his thanks to all those who have kindly supplied original photos and plans for reproduction, or have otherwise allowed their work to be reproduced. He owes a special debt to Dr. Ernest Nash and Generale Giulio Schmiedt, who have as always been generous with time, trouble, and helpful advice; and to Miss Sheila Gibson, who drew or redrew a number of the plans. He was also helped in preparing the illustrations by Miss Sue Bird and Miss Alison Howard-Drake.
Numbers refer to figure numbers.

Original photographs and plans:

E. Alföldi-Rosenbaum	28
American Academy in Rome	45
Antiquities Department of Algeria	65, 67
A. Boethius	86
British School at Rome	39, 44, 46, 52, 54–56, 58, 61, 63, 74a, 74b, 81
City of Zadar	78
Fotocielo	60
Fototeca dell'Unione	6, 66, 79, 80, 82, 85
S. S. Frere	69, 70
W. Froelich	27
S. Gibson	73
Pelican Books	77
J. K. St. Joseph	71
J. B. Ward-Perkins	68, 74

Derived from the following publications, in many cases with minor modifications and in several cases redrawn completely:

Altertümer von Pergamon, I (1912): 15
Annales (1970): 34, 35
Archäologischer Anzeiger (1962): 64
Athenische Mitteilungen, LXXIII (1955): 13
Bacon, Clarke, and Koldeway, *Investigations at Assos*, I (1901): 18, 19
R. Bohn, *Altertümer von Aegae* (1889): 16, 17
G. Boon, *Roman Silchester* (1957): 72
Bulletin des Etudes Orientales, IV (1935): 20
G. Carettoni *et al. La Pianta Marmorea di Roma Antica* (1960): 84
H. Eschebach, *Die Städtebauliche Entwicklung der antiken Pompeji* (1971): 41
Excavations at Dura-Europos: Ninth Season, 1 (1944): 22–25
Forma Italiae, III, 1: 36
Hesperia (successive reports): 3–5
G. Kleiner, *Die Ruinen von Milet* (1968): 9, 10
C. Kraeling, *Gerasa, City of the Decapolis* (1938): 26
R. Laur-Belart, *Führer durch Augusta Raurica*: 76
R. Martin, *L'urbanisme* (1950): 8
Mélanges de l'Ecole Française de Rome, LXXXIV. 1 (1972) (after Blawatskij): 37
Milet: Ergebnisse d. Ausgrabungen, II, 3 (1935): 7, 14
A. Piganiol, *Les documents cadastraux . . . d'Orange* (1962): 47, 48
Rend. Acc. Lincei, IX (1954): 43
David Robinson, *Olynthus*, XII (1946): 11, 11a
Scavi di Ostia, I (1953): 49, 50, 83
M. Schede, *Die Ruinen von Priene* (1954): 12a, 12b
G. Schmiedt, *Atlante Aerofotografico* (1970): 29–33, 38, 40, 42, 51, 57, 59, 62
F. Stähelin, *Die Schweiz in romischer Zeit* (1948): 75 (general plan)
Syria, XXVI (1949): 21
Town Planning Review, XXI (1950): 1, 2; XXVI (1955): 53
Wiegand and Schrade, *Priene* (1904): 12